Welcome!

English for the travel and tourism industry

Second Edition

Student's Book

Leo Jones

CAMBRIDGE
UNIVERSITY PRESS

CAMBRIDGE UNIVERSITY PRESS
Cambridge, New York, Melbourne, Madrid, Cape Town,
Singapore, São Paulo, Delhi, Mexico City

Cambridge University Press
The Edinburgh Building, Cambridge CB2 8RU, UK

www.cambridge.org
Information on this title: www.cambridge.org/9780521606592

First published 1998
Second edition 2005
11th printing 2013

Printed in Italy by L.E.G.O. S.p.A.

A catalogue record for this publication is available from the British Library

ISBN 978-0-521-60659-2 Student's Book
ISBN 978-0-521-60660-8 Teacher's Book
ISBN 978-0-521-60661-5 CD (audio) Set
ISBN 978-0-521-60662-2 cassette set

Cambridge University Press has no responsibility for the persistence or
accuracy of URLs for external or third-party internet websites referred to in
this publication, and does not guarantee that any content on such websites is,
or will remain, accurate or appropriate. Information regarding prices, travel
timetables and other factual information given in this work is correct at
the time of first printing but Cambridge University Press does not guarantee
the accuracy of such information thereafter.

Welcome!

Who is this course for?

Welcome! is for people in the travel and tourism industries who need (or will need) to use English when talking to clients: tourists, guests, visitors, customers or passengers.

Welcome! covers a wide range of different travel and tourism jobs and situations:

hotels • restaurants • cafés and bars • travel agencies • tour operators • information offices • airlines • cruise liners and ferries • rail and road transport • leisure facilities.

If you have to talk English to foreign visitors in your work, then **Welcome!** is for you!

How is the book organised?

There are 10 Modules in **Welcome!** and each contains 4 or 5 Lessons. Each Module is based on a different theme, and each Lesson covers a different aspect of the theme. Each lesson is divided into shorter sections containing different exercises and activities.

The Modules on more specialised themes (such as *Accommodation* or *Food and Drink*) are relevant for everyone, not only for people who are going to work in that particular area.

What does *Welcome!* contain?

The main focus of **Welcome!** is on speaking and listening, because these are the skills that are most important when dealing with clients. But you'll also have a chance to improve your reading and writing skills in some lessons. There are also lots of vocabulary exercises and some grammar review exercises.

Speaking   In many of the speaking activities you'll be working in pairs or in groups. These activities give you a chance to practise using English in discussions and in role plays where you can practise talking to clients. These activities help you to become more confident in speaking English.

Some role plays are 'Communication Activities', where each person looks at a different Activity.

The Activities are printed on different pages at the end of the book (pages 108–126). This means that you can't read each other's information, and a natural conversation develops between you.

It's important to use English all the time when you're working with partners – because the only way to improve your spoken English is by *speaking* it!

Before some role plays there's an exercise where you have to complete one side of a dialogue in writing before trying it yourself. There are pronunciation exercises to help you to speak in a clear, polite and friendly way.

Listening   The recordings for **Welcome!** include many different voices speaking at their natural speed. This will help you to understand different people when they speak to you in English. The questions in the book will help you to understand the main points the speakers make.

Vocabulary   **Welcome!** will help you to enrich your vocabulary. When you come across a useful new word or expression in the book, you should highlight it (using a fluorescent highlighter). This will help you to remember the new words you meet, so that you can use them yourself.

Reading   **Welcome!** includes reading texts from different sources, with questions to help you to understand them. There are also letters, emails and faxes from clients for you to read and act upon.

Writing   **Welcome!** includes Writing tasks which help you to improve your writing skills, so that you can write letters, emails and faxes to clients.

Welcome! includes advice on how to deal with clients.

Thank you for reading this introduction. Enjoy using **Welcome!**

Thanks

I'd like to thank everyone whose hard work, fresh ideas, helpful comments and criticisms have enhanced this book immensely.

The following teachers tried out the pilot lessons and reported on their experiences using them with their students:

Núria Cáceres in Sabadell, Spain; Jennyfer Chai-Chang in Valencia, Spain; Rose Cheung in Hong Kong; Suzanna Harwood in Athens, Greece; Patrick Lawlor in London; Mary Mumford de De Santiago in Guadalajara, Mexico; Bill Pellowe and Jayne Feldart in Fukuoka, Japan; Robin Walker in Oviedo, Spain; Nursel Yalçin in Aydin, Turkey

The following teachers reported on the pilot lessons:

Maud Dunkeld in the UK; Josette Hober-Ondersuhu in Grenoble, France; Antoinette Meehan in Tokyo, Japan; Inge Spaughton in Stuttgart, Germany; Gabriella Tavella in San Martin de los Andes, Argentina

Will Capel inititated the project and guided it through its many stages

Tony Garside edited the book and guided the project efficiently and sympathetically through to publication

Tim Douglass produced and edited the recordings

Stephanie White designed the Revised Edition at Kamae Design

And thanks to the people who took part in the interviews:

Sally Garside; Jane Sparkes; Janine Cording at AOSSA Travel in Brighton; Fiona Bowers and Sam Wilkinson at Dig in the Ribs in Brighton; Rob Allan, Emma Bray, Mark Fancy, Lisa Thomas and Emma Whiting at the Grand Hotel, Brighton.

Tony Robinson and Annemarie Young edited the Revised Edition. Thanks to them both!

Acknowledgements

The author and publishers are grateful to the authors, publishers and others who have given permission for the use of copyright material identified in the text. It has not always been possible to identify the source of material used or to contact the copyright holders and in such cases the publishers would welcome information from the copyright owners.

American Hotel & Motel Association for 'Traveler Safety Tips', p. 92; Fred Capel for the Chez Fred flyer, p. 47; CartoonStock for all cartoons; Dollar Rent A Car Systems, Inc., Tulsa, Oklahoma, USA for 'Welcome to Florida', p. 85; First Choice Holidays & Flights Ltd for the car hire information from First Choice Greece, p. 83; InterContinental Hotels Group for 'Reminders to Staff', p. 11 and for the example of a Holiday Inn Breakfast Order, pp. 36–37; Ian L. McQueen for the extract from Japan: A Budget Travel Guide, p. 74; Kuoni for the extracts from their brochure on p. 65 and p.125; Pangor Laut Resort, Malaysia for extracts and photographs from their brochure, p. 67; Spanish Tourist Office for their advertisement, p. 100; The Daily Telegraph for the extract from ' Mediterranean diet is the way to eat and drink your way to health'© Telegraph Group Limited, 19 September 2000, p. 44; 'Thai Airways International for their advertisement, p. 101.

For permission to include photographs:

Britstock-IFA, p.16*bc* (Eric Bach); Will Capel, p.21*br*, p.27 (3), p.38*t*, p.74*br*, p.84*r*; J Allan Cash, p.21*t*, p.29*l*, p.97*t*, p.103*b*, p.103*t*, p.105*tl*, p.105*tr*, p.105*br*; Trevor Clifford Photography, p.102; Comstock, p.43*t*, p.82, p.96*tr*, p.96*br*, p.103*tl*, p.105*bl*; Corbis, p.10*r*; p.28*tl*, p.28*tr*, p.30, p.32, p.39*tr*, p.39*bc*, p.78, p.80; Tim Douglass, p.8*l*, *cl*, *r*; Getty Images, p.9 (Stone), p.10*l* (Stone), p.14 (Stone), p.16*l* (Taxi), p.21*l* (Taxi), p.28*c* (Stone), p.38*cr* (Stone), p.38*b* (5, Foodpix), p.39*tl* (Foodpix), p.39*tr*, p.39*bl*, p.39*bc*, p.39*br*, p.42 (5, Foodpix), p.58, p.63 (Taxi), p.71 (Photographer's Choice), p.76, p.84*l* (Stone), p.97*c* (John Lamb), p.97*b* (Denis Waugh); Inverness Estate Limited, Papakura, New Zealand, p33*l*; Japan National Tourist Organization, p74*l*; Leo Jones, p.47, p.70, p.96*c*; Kingfish Lodge, Northland, New Zealand, p.33*r*; Kuoni Travel Ltd, p.65*t* (Steve Lucas), p.65*br* (Steve Lucas), p.65*bl* (Steve Lucas); Life File Photographic p.16*tc* (Jeremy Hoare), p.16*r* (Emma Lee); Le Meridien Hotels and Resorts, p29*r*; People 1st, p.10*c* ; Seaco Picture Library, p36; Rob Tomlinson, p.8*cr*, p.94*t*, 100*bt*; Travel Ink, p.40; John Walmsley, p.88 (4)

Illustrators:

Pantelis Palios p. 73; Bill Piggins pp. 12, 46, 61, 81, 89; Jamie Sneddon pp. 22*tl*, 24, 25*t*, 27*t*, 65*tl*, 76, 84, 86, 104, 115, 123; Kath Walker pp. 31, 64, 77, 93; Celia Witchard pp. 13, 15, 19, 35, 45, 51, 53, 55, 62, 68, 69, 88, 90, 98, 99, 107

p. = page, *t* = top, *c* = centre, *b* = bottom, *l* = left, *r* = right

Picture research by Sally Smith

Contents

Accommodation

Money

Travelling around

Problems

Attractions and activities

Communication activities

1 Working in travel and tourism

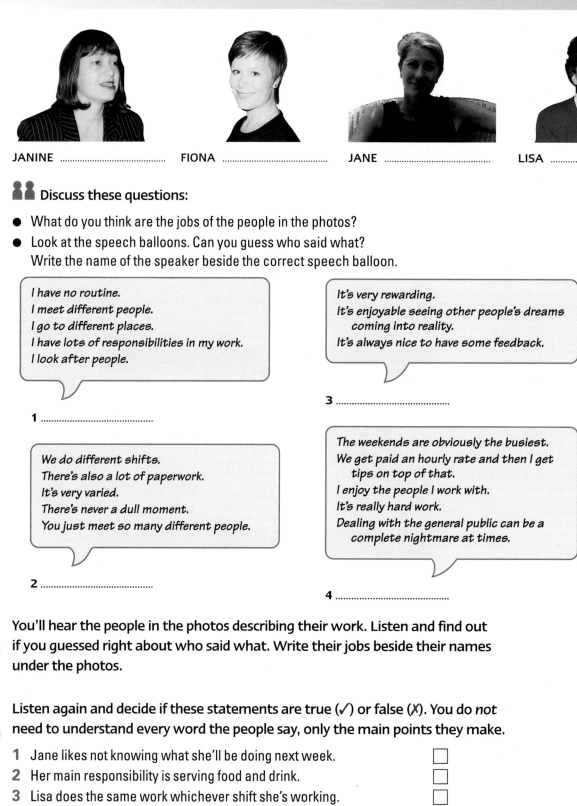

JANINE .... FIONA .... JANE .... LISA ....

A1 👥 Discuss these questions:

● What do you think are the jobs of the people in the photos?
● Look at the speech balloons. Can you guess who said what?
  Write the name of the speaker beside the correct speech balloon.

> *I have no routine.*
> *I meet different people.*
> *I go to different places.*
> *I have lots of responsibilities in my work.*
> *I look after people.*

1 ....

> *It's very rewarding.*
> *It's enjoyable seeing other people's dreams coming into reality.*
> *It's always nice to have some feedback.*

3 ....

> *We do different shifts.*
> *There's also a lot of paperwork.*
> *It's very varied.*
> *There's never a dull moment.*
> *You just meet so many different people.*

2 ....

> *The weekends are obviously the busiest.*
> *We get paid an hourly rate and then I get tips on top of that.*
> *I enjoy the people I work with.*
> *It's really hard work.*
> *Dealing with the general public can be a complete nightmare at times.*

4 ....

B1 🔊 You'll hear the people in the photos describing their work. Listen and find out if you guessed right about who said what. Write their jobs beside their names under the photos.

2 🔊 Listen again and decide if these statements are true (✓) or false (✗). You do *not* need to understand every word the people say, only the main points they make.

1 Jane likes not knowing what she'll be doing next week. ☐
2 Her main responsibility is serving food and drink. ☐
3 Lisa does the same work whichever shift she's working. ☐
4 She often gets the duty manager to help people who have complaints. ☐
5 Janine doesn't sell package tours, only flights. ☐
6 She doesn't often hear from her customers after their holiday. ☐
7 Fiona depends on tips to supplement her basic pay. ☐
8 She enjoys meeting her colleagues after work. ☐

C1  Look at the advertisement and discuss these questions:

- What does a local rep have to do?
- What are *three* things you might enjoy about the work?
- What are *three* things you would not enjoy about the work?

> He or she has to . . .
> It would be interesting to . . .
> It would be awful to have to . . .
> Something I wouldn't enjoy is . . .
> Another thing he or she has to do is . . .
> It would be awful to have to . . .
> Something I wouldn't enjoy is . . .

Utopia
HOLIDAYS

LOCAL RESORT REPRESENTATIVES

Utopia Holidays are looking for representatives in your region

The reps' duties will include:

- meeting clients at the airport and escorting them to their hotels
- holding welcome parties for each group on the day after their arrival
- organising and escorting coach excursions to local places of interest
- answering clients' questions and dealing with their problems
- assisting clients who cannot speak the local language
- escorting clients from their hotels to the airport at the end of their holiday
- being on call 24 hours a day to deal with emergencies

Please apply in writing, enclosing your CV, to
Alice Watson, Utopia Holidays, Utopia House, Skyway Drive, Crawley, RH12 4PJ

2 👥+👥 Compare your ideas.

3 Writing

Write about 50 words about the work you do (or will do).

Begin like this:

In my job I have to . . . or
In my job I'll probably have to . . .

> If you give clients the impression that you enjoy your work — and enjoy dealing with them — it will make it much easier for clients to feel comfortable with you. And it will make it easier for you to establish a good relationship with them. If you look bored or uninterested, your clients may start feeling the same. If you smile, other people will smile back!

2 Being friendly and helpful

A 👤👤👤👤 Find out about the last time your partners went to a restaurant, a café and a shop. Discuss these questions:

● How helpful and friendly were the staff?
● What did the staff do to make you feel welcome? What did they say to you?
● Would you recommend each place to a friend? Why/Why not?

> *The staff were really friendly but the food wasn't very good.*
> *The staff were rather unhelpful but the food was excellent.*

B1 🔊 You'll hear three conversations. Listen and decide which of the people in the photos sounds unfriendly and unhelpful.

 A    B    C

2 🔊 Listen again. Match the problems 1–3 and the places a–c to the conversations.

1 The client is nervous.   **a** at a reception desk
2 The guest hasn't had her order taken.   **b** at a check-in desk
3 The reservation hasn't been made.   **c** in a restaurant

	Problem	Place
Conversation 1	....	....
Conversation 2	....	....
Conversation 3	....	....

C1 👤👤 Cross out the phrases that might sound unfriendly or impolite, like the one crossed out.

Could you tell me your name please?   ~~Who are you?~~
What do you want?   May I help you?
It's a pleasure.   It's no trouble.
Certainly.   Obviously.
Do you want something?   Is there anything I can do for you?

2 Pronunciation

🔊 👤👤 Listen to three model dialogues. Then practise them, taking it in turns to play the roles of the CLIENT and a friendly, helpful MEMBER OF STAFF.

Good evening.
— *Good evening, sir. Can I help you?*
Yes, I'd like to send a fax, please.
— *Certainly, sir, would you like it sent right away?*

Good morning.
— *Good morning, sir. Can I help you?*
Yes, I'd like some information, please.
— *Certainly, sir.*

Good afternoon.
— *Good afternoon, madam. How may I help you?*
I'd like to book a table for this evening, please.
— *Certainly, madam, what time would you like it for?*

D1 👥 This document is a reminder to staff at a major hotel.
Which do you think are the three most important pieces of advice?

Speak to people:
there is nothing as nice as a cheerful word of greeting.

Smile at people:
it takes seventy-two muscles to frown, only fourteen to smile.

Call people by name:
the sweetest music to anyone's ears is the sound of their own name.

Be friendly:
you can make friends by being friendly.

Be helpful:
act as if everything is a genuine pleasure.

Be interested in people:
you can like everyone if you try.

Consider the feelings of others:
it will be appreciated.

---

2 👥+👥 Compare your ideas for D1. Then look at the answers to the
questions below. Number the statements in order of importance (1–4)
and explain why. Then add another answer for each question.

- I enjoy dealing with people because:
  - *I like meeting new people.* ☐
  - *people are usually very friendly.* ☐
  - *I find it challenging.* ☐
  - *every person you meet is different.* ☐

  ....

- I find the most difficult things in dealing with people are:
  - *it's hard to be friendly and helpful all the time.* ☐
  - *people aren't always appreciative.* ☐
  - *some people are difficult.* ☐
  - *people get impatient when they have to wait.* ☐

  ....

If you give people a favourable first impression of yourself, you'll find them much easier to deal with. A welcoming smile and a friendly greeting puts people at their ease, even if they have had a bad journey, or if they are feeling tired, worried or cross.

Remember: You never get a second chance to make a first impression!

3 When in Rome ...

A1 Read this description of how westerners should behave at a Japanese *ryokan* (traditional inn). Match the pictures A–G to the paragraphs 1–7.

Your first visit to a ryokan

The Japanese ryokan (traditional inn) is an experience that visitors should not overlook. Ryokan offer the best in Japanese food, service, and traditional atmosphere.

1 Before you step inside a *ryokan*, remove your shoes and put on a pair of slippers. Slippers are worn everywhere inside, except on the *tatami* matting, where you should walk in bare feet or in socks. You may need thick socks if the weather is cold.

2 In your room you sit on cushions called *zabuton* arranged around the low table. In the winter season, there may be a blanket around the table. You slip your feet under the blanket for the warmth of a *kotatsu* electrical heating unit. This is where your meals are served.

3 Your *futon* bedding is laid out on the floor. It consists of a mattress, sheets, a thick cover, and extra blankets if needed. A thin *yukata* robe is provided for you to wear. In cold weather there is also a *tanzen* gown to wear over it.

4 The toilet is usually Japanese style. You don't sit on it but squat over it, facing the hooded end. Special slippers are provided for use only in the toilet area.

5 Most ryokans have *ofuro* (communal bath) where you can meet your fellow-guests and chat to them. First you undress in the changing room and place your things in a basket. You take a towel to wrap around you and to dry yourself with.

6 Before you get into the bath, you must go to the washing area. Here you sit on a low stool in front of a pair of hot/cold water faucets. Fill a bath pan with water, and pour it over your body to get soaking wet all over. If there are no faucets, use a bath pan to scoop water from the bath. Use the shower while seated on the stool, never standing up. Soap and rinse off thoroughly. Only then do you get into the communal bath for a long, relaxing soak.

7 At an *onzen* (hot spring resort) there will be hot and cold baths. Here you can get really hot in a hot bath, then cool off in an ice-cold one. Very refreshing. There will also be a *roten-buro* (outdoor bath) where you can enjoy the fresh air while soaking in a hot bath. Lovely in cold weather with snow on the ground!

A   B   C   D   E   F   G

2 What do you think are the three most surprising or strangest things for someone who has never visited Japan? Highlight them or note them down.

3 👤+👤 Compare your ideas. Then discuss these questions:

- What do you think are the two most important things for a western visitor to remember in Japanese-style accommodation?
- What would you enjoy most about spending a night at a *ryokan*? What would you not enjoy?
- Where do you recommend that a visitor to your country should stay to get the best impression of everyday life there?
- What do you recommend to a first-time visitor to your country? Make a list of DOS and DON'TS.

B1 👥 Discuss each of these questions. Then tick (✓) what you think is the best answer to each question.

"When in Rome, do as the Romans do"

1 A man with a beard, wearing dirty jeans and carrying a rucksack comes into the 5-star hotel where you're working. What do you do?

a Ask him what he wants. ☐
b Ignore him. ☐
c Ask him politely to leave. ☐
d Treat him like any other guest. ☐

2 You know Ms Brown, an American client, very well. When she arrives do you …

a shake her hand? ☐
b smile and say *Hello*? ☐
c kiss her on the cheek? ☐
d say *Good evening* and bow? ☐

3 Mr Manuel Fernandez Garcia doesn't reply when you say "*Good morning, Mr Garcia*" to him. This is probably because …

a he didn't hear you. ☐
b you didn't look at him when you spoke. ☐
c he's rudely ignoring you. ☐
d you've called him by the wrong name. ☐

4 A German is talking to a Brazilian. The German keeps taking a step backwards each time the Brazilian steps forward. This is probably because …

a the Brazilian wants to be too friendly. ☐
b they're both trying to be friendly. ☐
c the German is being unfriendly. ☐
d they don't like each other. ☐

5 You are talking to a visitor from Britain. Which of these questions do you ask him or her?

a *How old are you?* ☐
b *How much do you earn?* ☐
c *Are you married?* ☐
d *What part of Britain do you come from?* ☐

2 👥+👥 Compare your answers. Can you think of any more examples of misunderstandings that might arise when dealing with people from other countries?

Just because a person comes from a particular country, don't assume they'll behave like a 'typical' person from that country — whatever you imagine that to be! Treat each person as an individual.

Unless you know a foreign guest really well, don't treat them too informally as they might think you're being over-familiar or even insincere. Different nationalities have different customs when it comes to formality and informality.

4 Dealing with enquiries

A1 You'll hear three short conversations in which clients are asking for information. The first time you listen, tick (✓) the boxes to show the right answers. The second time you listen, fill the blanks in the sentences.

1a The first guest wants to know about …
a room for himself. ☐   a room for someone else. ☐

1b He is told that Room .... is free.

2a The second guest wants to know how long it takes to get to the airport …
by bus. ☐   by taxi. ☐

2b She is told that she has to check in at least .... minutes before her flight.

3a The third guest wants to know what time …
breakfast service begins. ☐   breakfast service finishes. ☐

3b He is told that breakfast is served from .... to .... on weekdays and from .... to .... at weekends.

2 Listen again and tick (✓) the boxes to show which phrases in the speech balloons are used by the receptionist.

Good evening. How can I help you? ☐
How nice to see you again! ☐
Hello again, Mr Grey! How are you today? ☐
It's really nice to see you again! ☐
Welcome back! ☐
I hope you enjoy your stay with us! ☐

Good morning. What can I do for you? ☐
Is there anything else I can do for you? ☐
Have an enjoyable day! ☐
Have a good day! ☐
You're welcome! ☐
You're very welcome. ☐
It's a pleasure. ☐

👥 When would you say the phrases in the first balloon?
When would you say the ones in the second balloon?

B 1   Complete this dialogue with suitable words. You may be able to use some of the phrases in the speech balloons opposite.

RECEPTIONIST: *Good afternoon, Mr Johnson. How nice to see you again!* ....

GUEST: Thank you, it's very nice to be here again. How are you?

RECEPTIONIST: ....

GUEST: Good. Now, I asked for my usual room when I made the booking. Is it available?

RECEPTIONIST: ....

GUEST: Oh, well, never mind. Room 101 does overlook the garden too, doesn't it ?

RECEPTIONIST: ....

GUEST: Oh, until Friday I expect. But is it all right if I let you know for sure tomorrow morning?

RECEPTIONIST: ....

GUEST: Good. Thanks very much. Don't worry about a porter. I've only got this small overnight bag.

RECEPTIONIST: ....

2   Pronunciation

Listen to the model version of the dialogue. Then practise it, taking it in turns to play the roles of the RECEPTIONIST and the GUEST. Make sure you sound as friendly and helpful as possible.

C   Role play

One of you should look at Activity 1 on page 108, one at Activity 17 on page 116 and the other(s) at Activity 33 on page 124.

This activity consists of six short role plays. In each role play there are two roles: GUEST or MEMBER OF STAFF. There is also an OBSERVER, who listens to the role play and then gives the others feedback on how polite and friendly they sounded.

You can make people feel welcome and help them to feel at home by using their names instead of addressing them impersonally as *Sir* or *Madam*. Look for clues on credit cards, forms, luggage labels, etc. Make sure they know *your* name too, and show them that you remember their names when you meet them again.

A sincere smile shows people that you want to be friendly. Good eye contact shows that you're interested in them. Try to treat every client in the same way that you'd like to be treated yourself — or even better!

5 Different ways of travelling

A 👥👥👥👥 Look at the photos and discuss these questions:

- Which of the modes of transport have you used?
- Which is your favourite? Why?
- Which is/would be the worst, as far as you're concerned? Why?

B1 **Grammar** *can/can't, have to and should/shouldn't*

Decide which of the activities in this list are allowed or not allowed, and which are
encouraged or discouraged on a . . .

> plane   ship   train   long-distance bus or coach

smoking	drinking alcohol	standing up during the journey
opening the window	wearing a seat belt	showing your ticket to the conductor
travelling without a ticket	singing songs	annoying the other passengers
getting drunk	talking to the driver	remaining seated during the journey

On a ship you can smoke but you can't travel without a ticket.
On a long-distance bus you can't . . . and you have to . . .
On a train you should . . . but you shouldn't . . .

2 👥👥 Write six sentences in total about the four modes of transport, using *can*,
can't, *have to*, *should* or *shouldn't*.

3 👥👥+👥👥 Compare your sentences.

C There are 10 mistakes in this article. Find the mistakes and correct them – the first is done for you as an example!

Afraid of flying?
It doesn't need to take over your life

engines

A third of us are afraid of flying. For most people flying is a strange mixture of anxiety and excitement. Is this how you feel?

You strap yourself into your seat, take a deep breath and close your eyes. The ~~passengers~~ start to roar, the plane races down the runway, going faster and faster until, at the last minute, it climbs slowly into the clouds. Now all you can do is stand for hours on end, squashed in a narrow seat, unable to move, unable to see where you are going. During the flight there may be turbulence, when the plane bounces around in the sky. There's no chance of escape until the worst moment of all: landing. Eventually the doors open and you step outside and you're safe again.

Is it best never to leave the ground, and travel everywhere by land or sea? Or are there ways of training yourself to be less afraid of flying?

Here are some thoughts which might reassure you:
- Flying is much safer than travelling by air
- Plenty of people (pilots, flight attendants, engineers) spend their working lives flying day in day out and they retire after a lifetime of flying

If you know what's going on during a flight (and why) you'll feel less afraid. Fear is often due to ignorance. Before you fly, find out the answers to these questions:
- How does a plane stay in the air?
- Why does the engine noise change sometimes?
- What causes turbulence and how does it happen?
- Is it dangerous to fly through a thunderstorm?
- How can the drivers see where they're going when it's cloudy?

Reduce stress before the flight. Try to feel more relaxed generally. Here are some ideas to reduce stress:
- Leave plenty of time the day before you travel to pack and get yourself organized
- Have a good night's sleep the night after you fly
- Spend the night before an early flight at the airport hotel
- Make sure you have your tickets and passport safely packed in your carry-on bag
- Make sure you have plenty of things to read in case there are delays

- Arrive at the airport a long time before you have to check out
- Check in early so that you can choose where to sit – you feel turbulence more at the back of the aircraft, so choose a seat near the back
- Find a quiet comfortable place to sit and relax in the departure lounge
- Have something to eat. It may be quite a while before you get a meal on the plane. But don't have a big meal
- Don't drink alcohol – it will help you relax and it will dehydrate you

When you do get on the plane, don't sit worrying:
- Sit down, unfasten your seat belt, read the safety instructions
- Watch the safety demonstration carefully
- Take long, deep, slow breaths
- Relax by tightening each group of muscles. Start with your toes and work up to your face – don't forget your fingers and arms.
- Read a book or magazine
- If there's movie, watch it. It will take your mind off your worries
- Keep your seat belt loosely fastened during the flight

If all else fails, take a Fear of Flying course. Two ex-British Airways pilots run Aviatours, which specializes in Fear of Flying courses. After time in the classroom, you go up in a real plane. Their success rate is very low, apparently.

D1 👥 Compare your answers – did you find all 10 mistakes? What are the five most useful pieces of advice in the article?

2 Role play

👥 Take turns to play the roles of a travel agent and a client who is afraid of flying.

6 Asking questions

A1 👥 Here are some questions that might be asked at a travel agent's.
Match the replies a–h to the client's questions 1–8.

1 *Do I have to change planes anywhere?*
2 *Can I get an APEX ticket?*
3 *Is it best to fly from Paris to Lyon?*
4 *I'm booked on a flight to New York tomorrow, but I can't travel then. What should I do?*
5 *What time do I have to be at the airport?*
6 *Does the flight stop anywhere en route?*
7 *Does the train go all the way to Venice?*
8 *How much is a round trip ticket to Tokyo?*

a *Is that economy class or business class?*
b *No, it's a direct flight.*
c *No, it's a non-stop flight.*
d *No, you have to change trains in Bologna. Is that OK?*
e *Not really, it's better to take a train.*
f *Would you like me to cancel your reservation?*
g *Yes, but only if you stay over Saturday night. Is that all right?*
h *Your check-in time is 05.30 and your departure time is 06.30. Do you want me to book you a taxi?*

2 🔊 You'll hear eight short dialogues. Listen and decide which of the people (including the clients) did *not* speak politely.

B1 Grammar *Questions*

On the right are the responses to some questions. What were the questions?
Fill the blanks.

	Question	Response
1	*What time does your flight leave?*	It leaves at 7.45.
2	.... check in?	I have to be there 90 minutes before.
3	.... people .... in your party?	There are four of us including myself.
4	.... your full name?	John Albert Smith.
5	.... room .... ?	I'd like a double room with balcony.
6	.... ?	I'll be leaving on Monday morning.
7	.... ?	I'm going to pay by Visa.
8	.... ?	I'd like a call at 7am please.

2 Pronunciation

🔊 👥 Listen to the model questions. Then practise the questions and answers, taking it in turns to play the roles of the CLIENT and the TRAVEL AGENT. Make sure you sound as polite as possible.

3 Role play

👥 Unjumble the sentences in the speech balloon to make questions. Then imagine that one of you is a VISITOR from another country and the other is asking about the visitor's country. Find out more about the country, using the unjumbled questions. Change roles.

How been have you long country this in?
How spend time here going to are you much?
What do come country you from part of the?
What food kind of popular in most is country your?
What time have usually people do dinner?
When close stores the on do a weekday?
Where country your in tourists most do go?
Which region most beautiful the is?
Who country's president/prime minister your is?
Why visiting your country enjoy do tourists?
What country you come did to this for?

C *Could you tell me ...?* questions often sound more polite than direct questions, especially if the question is personal, difficult or annoying.

1 Look at these examples and notice the word order in each question. Then do exercise 2 below.

Direct Questions	Could you tell me ...?
When are you leaving?	*Could you tell me when you're leaving?*
How long are you going to stay?	*Could you tell me how long you're going to stay?*
What is your date of birth?	*Could you tell me what your date of birth is?*
What is your first name?	*Could you tell me what your first name is?*

2 Imagine that you're talking to a guest. Think of suitable *Could you tell me ...?* questions to ask.

1 My name is difficult to spell.
2 I'm leaving soon.
3 I arrived in this country recently.
4 I gave my tickets to someone.
5 I'm leaving early next week.
6 My suit needs pressing.
7 I want to see the manager.

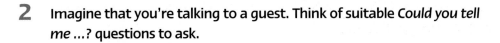

Could you tell me how *you spell your name* ?
Could you tell me when *you're leaving* ?
Could you tell me when .... ?
Could you tell me who .... ?
Could you tell me which day .... ?
Could you tell me when .... ?
Could you tell me why .... ?

D1 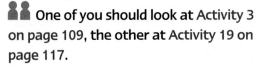 Read this letter to guests at a hotel and discuss these questions:

● Why are questionnaires useful for hotels?
● Why should guests bother to complete them?

2 Role play

 One of you should look at Activity 3 on page 109, the other at Activity 19 on page 117.

Play the roles of GUEST and MEMBER OF STAFF. Imagine that you're doing a guest survey, to find out more about the guest's reactions to your hotel.

A special questionnaire for our guests

Dear Guest,

Your ideas on what we can do to continuously improve our hotel are very important to us.

It is our goal to satisfy the needs of our customers and exceed their expectations.

Therefore it would be very much appreciated if you could take a little time to complete this questionnaire.

Thank you for staying with us.

We hope you enjoyed your stay with us and will return soon.

Yours sincerely,

7 Taking a booking

A You'll hear a travel agent dealing with a client. Listen and note down the client's requirements on the form.

- The travel agent forgot to ask one thing. What was it?

RETURN FLIGHT FROM		TO
DATE AND TIME OF OUTWARD FLIGHT		
DATE AND TIME OF RETURN FLIGHT		
NUMBER OF PASSENGERS		
TYPE OR CLASS OF FARE		
PREFERRED AIRLINE		
METHOD OF PAYMENT		
NAME		
ADDRESS		
TELEPHONE NUMBER		

B Complete this dialogue with appropriate questions. Then listen and compare your questions with the model version.

TRAVEL AGENT:	*Good morning, sir. How may I help you?*
CLIENT:	Good morning. Can I make an airline reservation, please?
TRAVEL AGENT:	.... ?
CLIENT:	From Athens to Istanbul.
TRAVEL AGENT:	.... ?
CLIENT:	I'd like to leave Athens on the 2nd of next month, returning on the 13th.
TRAVEL AGENT:	.... ?
CLIENT:	I'd like to arrive in Istanbul by lunchtime, and be back in Athens by dinnertime.
TRAVEL AGENT:	.... ?
CLIENT:	There'll be three of us — two adults and one child.
TRAVEL AGENT:	.... ?
CLIENT:	She's eight years old.
TRAVEL AGENT:	.... ?
CLIENT:	Economy class — the cheapest fares you can get, if possible!
TRAVEL AGENT:	.... ?
CLIENT:	No, I don't mind which airline it is.
TRAVEL AGENT:	All right, I'll just check the computer to find out about availability …

C Role play

👥 One of you should look at Activity 5 on page 110, the other at Activity 20 on page 118.

You'll be playing the roles of TRAVEL AGENT and CLIENT and filling out this reservation form for a holiday in the USA. This role play is in two parts.

			DEPARTURE DATE		DEPARTURE AIRPORT	NUMBER OF FLIGHTS
MR/MRS/ MISS/MS	INITIALS	SURNAME		HOLIDAY INSURANCE	ADDRESS OF FIRST PERSON NAMED TO WHOM ALL CORRESPONDENCE WILL BE SENT	
				YES/NO		
				YES/NO		
				YES/NO		
				YES/NO		
				YES/NO		

HOTELS		NUMBER OF NIGHTS	ARRIVAL DATE	ROOM TYPE	NUMBER OF ROOMS	ROOM SUPPLEMENT OR EXTRAS

SPECIAL REQUEST (HONEYMOON/DIET etc)

IMPORTANT Client's Emergency Telephone numbers in case of strikes, delays, re-routing etc.
HOME: OTHER:

8 The best way to get there

BA	British Airways
BD	bmi
SN	SN Brussels Airlines
TV	Virgin Express
LCY	London City Airport
LGW	London Gatwick
LHR	London Heathrow
1	Monday
7	Sunday

From LONDON

day	dep.	arr.	airport	flight
To BRUSSELS National				
12345--	0650	0900	LHR	BD141
1234567	0655	0905	LHR	BA388
12345--	0805	1005	LCY	TV2952
123456-	0825	1035	LHR	BD145
12345--	0845	1050	LGW	SN2122
1234567	0855	1100	LHR	BA392
1234567	1100	1315	LHR	BA402
12345--	1120	1320	LCY	TV2954
12345--	1130	1330	LHR	SN601
123456-	1205	1420	LHR	BD149
1234567	1220	1430	LHR	BA394
------7	1250	1500	LHR	BD149
1234567	1545	1755	LHR	BA396
12345--	1430	1630	LCY	TV2956
12345--	1430	1640	LHR	BD151
1234567	1625	1835	LHR	BD153
12345-7	1730	1930	LGW	SN2130
12345-7	1745	1950	LCY	TV2958
1234567	1745	1955	LHR	BA398
12345--	1820	2030	LHR	BD155
123456-	2015	2225	LHR	BD157
12345--	2045	2245	LCY	TV2960

To LONDON

day	dep.	arr.	airport	flight
From BRUSSELS National				
123456-	0720	0740	LHR	BD140
12345--	0725	0735	LCY	TV2951
1234567	0740	0800	LHR	BA389
12345--	0745	0745	LGW	SN2123
12345--	0900	0940	LHR	SN600
12345--	0945	1005	LHR	BD142
12345--	1045	1050	LCY	TV2953
1234567	1045	1105	LHR	BA393
1234567	1120	1135	LHR	BD146
1234567	1250	1300	LHR	BA403
1234567	1345	1400	LHR	BA395
12345--	1400	1400	LCY	TV2955
123456-	1500	1510	LHR	BD150
------7	1540	1550	LHR	BD150
12345--	1650	1650	LGW	SN2129
12345--	1715	1715	LCY	TV2957
1234567	1720	1730	LHR	BA397
12345--	1720	1735	LHR	BD152
1234567	1915	1930	LHR	BD154
1234567	1915	1935	LHR	BA399
123457-	2015	2015	LCY	TV2959
12345--	2110	2125	LHR	BD156

eurostar

MONDAY ➤ SATURDAY

Brussels Midi/Zuid ➤ London Waterloo

dep	arr	train	days
07.25	09.01	9111	12345--
07.25	08.59	9111	-----6-
07.56	09.35	9113	------7
08.56	10.24	9117	123456-
11.01	12.28	9125	123456-
11.01	12.32	9125	------7
12.58	14.25	9133	1234567
14.56	16.25	9141	1234567
17.01	18.30	9149	12345-7
17.56	19.28	9153	1234567
19.56	21.27	9161	12345--
20.26	21.56	9163	-----67

London Waterloo ➤ Brussels Midi/Zuid

dep	arr	train	days
06.26	10.01	9108	-----6-
06.29	10.01	9108	12345--
08.34	12.10	9116	------7
08.39	12.10	9116	123456-
10.37	14.05	9124	------7
10.42	14.05	9124	123456-
12.34	16.10	9132	------7
12.39	16.10	9132	123456-
14.42	18.02	9140	1234567
16.39	20.10	9148	1234567
18.11	21.37	9154	12345--
18.39	22.10	9156	-----67
19.39	23.10	9160	12345-7

Cambridge is 1 hour by train from London King's Cross or Liverpool Street

Brighton is 30 mins by train from Gatwick or 1 hour from London Victoria

Gatwick Express takes 30 minutes to London Victoria

Heathrow Express takes 15 minutes to London Paddington

London Underground from Heathrow takes 1 hour to Central London and King's Cross

Thameslink trains from Heathrow to King's Cross take 1 hour

The shuttle bus from London City takes 15 minutes to Canary Wharf and 30 mins to Liverpool Street

Waterloo to Canary Wharf is 15 minutes by Underground

A1 Grammar If . . .

Fill the blanks using these words: arrive   catch   depart   leave   get   fly   reach   take

1 If Mr A *catches* the Eurostar train at 8.56, *he'll get* to Waterloo at *10.24*.

2 If he .... from Brussels at 7.40 on BA, he ...... at Heathrow at ....

3 If you .... the SN flight at 9.00, you ...... to Heathrow at ....

4 If you .... Brussels at 12:58 by train, you ...... at Waterloo at ....

5 If you .... the last flight from Brussels, you ...... at Heathrow at ....

6 If you want to .... London before 9 am, you ....

2 Here are requests for information from four clients who want to travel from Brussels to England. Decide together what advice to give them.

Mr A wants to get to Canary Wharf in London's Docklands by 11am. What is the best way to get there?

Ms B wants to get to Brighton before lunch. What is the best way to get there?

Mr C wants to reach Cambridge in time to check in at his hotel and freshen up before dinner at 8 pm. What is the best way to get there?

Ms D wants to get to her hotel at London Heathrow on Saturday night. What is the best way to get there and does she have time to have dinner in Brussels?

VOYAGES GULLIVER S.A.

Local time in Brussels is one hour later than London. (Central European Time / Greenwich Mean Time)

ITINERARY
FOR MR ALAN WATSON

MON 13 MAR	REPORT TO SABENA, BRUSSELS NATIONAL BY 0830				
MON 13 MAR	DEP	BRUSSELS NATIONAL	0930	SABENA	SN 600
MON 13 MAR	ARR	LONDON HEATHROW	0940	RESERVATION IS CONFIRMED IN BUSINESS CLASS	

CONFIRMED ROOM RESERVATION FROM 13-14 MAR AT SHERLOCK HOLMES HOTEL, LONDON

TUE 14 MAR	REPORT TO QANTAS, LONDON HEATHROW TERMINAL 3 BY 1015				
TUE 14 MAR	DEP	LONDON HEATHROW	1215	QANTAS	QF 002
WED 15 MAR	ARR	SYDNEY	2045	RESERVATION IS CONFIRMED IN BUSINESS CLASS	

CONFIRMED ROOM RESERVATION FROM 15-21 MAR AT PLAZA HOTEL, SYDNEY

TUE 21 MAR	REPORT TO QANTAS, SYDNEY INTERNATIONAL TERMINAL BY 2045				
TUE 21 MAR	DEP	SYDNEY	2215	QANTAS	QF 021
WED 22 MAR	ARR	TOKYO	0640	RESERVATION IS CONFIRMED IN BUSINESS CLASS	

CONFIRMED ROOM RESERVATION FROM 21-26 MAR AT HILLTOP HOTEL, TOKYO

SUN 26 MAR	REPORT TO OLYMPIC AIRWAYS, TOKYO NARITA TERMINAL 2 BY 2130				
SUN 26 MAR	DEP	TOKYO NARITA	2130	OLYMPIC	OA 478
MON 27 MAR	ARR	ATHENS	0805	RESERVATION IS CONFIRMED IN BUSINESS CLASS	
MON 27 MAR	DEP	ATHENS	0910	RESERVATION IS CONFIRMED IN BUSINESS CLASS	
TUE 28 MAR	ARR	BRUSSELS	1130		

B1 Look at the itinerary and check it for mistakes. (There are two mistakes in it.)

2 Listen to the travel agent as she explains the itinerary to her client. Find out if the two mistakes are spotted by the client.

3 Listen to the way the travel agent explains each step of the route. This will help you to do the role play in 4 more easily. Which of the phrases in the speech balloon does she use?

> I'll just go through the itinerary with you . . .
> First of all . . .
> After that . . .
> You have to check in at . . .
> There's a misprint here. It should say . . .
> Make sure that you reconfirm your tickets when you arrive in . . .
> I hope you enjoy your trip!

4 Role play

One of you should look at Activity 2 on page 108, the other at Activity 18 on page 116.

You'll be playing the roles of TRAVEL AGENT and CLIENT.
This role play is in two parts.

9 Around the world

A Vocabulary *countries and nationalities*

👥 Match the names of these countries to their flags below.
Then write down the nationality of a person from each country.

USA .....*1 — American*..... UK .....*2 — British*..... Australia ....

Austria .... Belgium .... Canada ....

France .... Germany .... Greece ....

Hungary .... Italy .... Japan ....

Malaysia .... Mexico .... the Netherlands ....

South Africa .... Spain .... Sweden ....

Switzerland .... Thailand .... Turkey ....

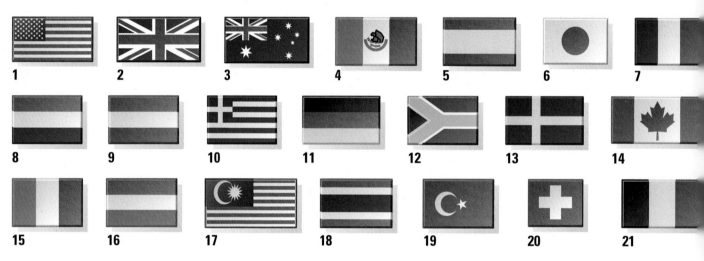

B1 Pronunciation ABC

👥 Which of these airport codes can you match to the cities on the
map opposite? Make sure you say the letters clearly.

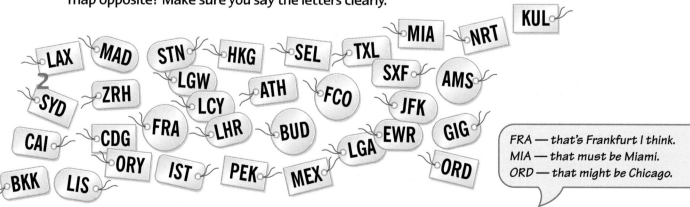

FRA — *that's Frankfurt I think.*
MIA — *that must be Miami.*
ORD — *that might be Chicago.*

2 Find out if you guessed right. One of you should look at Activity 6 on
page 110, the other at Activity 21 on page 118.

24

C1 Grammar *If . . .*

Which of the countries would you visit if you could afford it, and what would you do there? Write *five* sentences about five of the countries you'd like to visit.

If I had enough money, I'd travel to America. I'd visit New York and go up the Empire State Building.
If I could afford it, I'd go to .... I'd visit ....

2 👤+👤 Compare your sentences and ask your partner to explain *why* he or she would like to go to each place.

D1 👥 Imagine you could go on a round-the-world trip visiting ten different cities. Plan your route. You must fly *westwards* from your nearest international airport and the complete trip must last 28 days.

2 👥+👥 Tell each other about your routes, and give your reasons.

> We'd start at . . . and then fly on to. . . where we'd stop for . . . days. After that we'd go to . . .

FREQUENT FLYER CLASS (EXCUSED SAFETY DEMO)

10 Organising a trip

A1 👥👥 Read this email from your client, Ms Mary Rivers. She is an American businessperson who is based in Madrid. What does she want you to do?

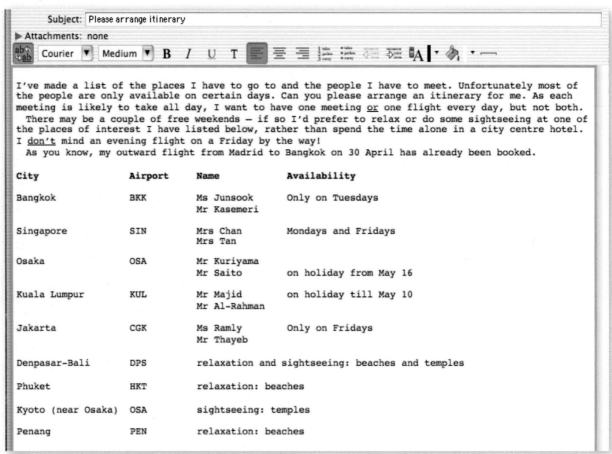

Subject: Please arrange itinerary

Attachments: none

I've made a list of the places I have to go to and the people I have to meet. Unfortunately most of the people are only available on certain days. Can you please arrange an itinerary for me. As each meeting is likely to take all day, I want to have one meeting <u>or</u> one flight every day, but not both.
  There may be a couple of free weekends — if so I'd prefer to relax or do some sightseeing at one of the places of interest I have listed below, rather than spend the time alone in a city centre hotel. I <u>don't</u> mind an evening flight on a Friday by the way!
  As you know, my outward flight from Madrid to Bangkok on 30 April has already been booked.

City	Airport	Name	Availability
Bangkok	BKK	Ms Junsook Mr Kasemeri	Only on Tuesdays
Singapore	SIN	Mrs Chan Mrs Tan	Mondays and Fridays
Osaka	OSA	Mr Kuriyama Mr Saito	on holiday from May 16
Kuala Lumpur	KUL	Mr Majid Mr Al-Rahman	on holiday till May 10
Jakarta	CGK	Ms Ramly Mr Thayeb	Only on Fridays
Denpasar-Bali	DPS	relaxation and sightseeing: beaches and temples	
Phuket	HKT	relaxation: beaches	
Kyoto (near Osaka)	OSA	sightseeing: temples	
Penang	PEN	relaxation: beaches	

2 Use the information opposite to help you to plan her trip. Complete the itinerary below with the details of the trip. Include the days she will have meetings and with whom.

ITINERARY FOR:
MS MARY RIVERS
PLEASE CHECK IN AT MADRID BARAJAS BY 10.40 ON SUNDAY APRIL 30

DATE	FROM	TO	FLIGHT	DEP	ARR	DATE
30 APRIL	MADRID	BANGKOK	TG943	12:40	08:30	1 MAY

2 May Meeting with Ms Junsook in Bangkok

3 👥👥+👥👥 Compare your itineraries. Which one seems better? Why?

B Writing

Write the letter you'll send to Ms Rivers to accompany the itinerary, explaining the reasons for the routes you've chosen.

MAY

Su	M	Tu	W	Th	F	Sa
30	1	2	3	4	5	6
7	8	9	10	11	12	13
14	15	16	17	18	19	20
21	22	23	24	25	26	27
28	29	30	31	1	2	3

BKK → CGK

1135	1630
1800	2130

CGK → BKK

0800	1130
1740	2235

BKK → DPS

1030	1535

DPS → BKK

1700	2000

BKK → KUL

1140	1440
1910	2210

KUL → BKK

1000	1100
1510	1610

BKK → HKT

1000	1120
1800	1920
2100	2220

HKT → BKK

1050	1215
1510	1635
1910	2035

BKK → MAD

2359	1010

MAD → BKK

1240	0830

BKK → OSA

0915	1635
2359	0730

OSA → BKK

1145	1530
1925	2300

BKK → SIN

1030	1245
1915	2115

SIN → BKK

1015	1215
1820	2020

CGK → DPS

0900	1000
1830	2030

DPS → CGK

1100	1200
1910	2020

KUL → CGK

1230	1305
2000	2035

CGK → KUL

1130	1400
1800	2030

KUL → OSA

1000	1715
2330	0615

OSA → KUL

0945	1430
1805	2300

KUL → PEN

1100	1130
2000	2030

PEN → KUL

0800	0830
2100	2130

SIN → CGK

0900	0935
1300	1330
1800	1830

CGK → SIN

0930	1200
1330	1600
1730	2000

SIN → DPS

0910	1135
1640	1905

DPS → SIN

1745	2005
2005	2225

SIN → MAD

1030	0900
1735	1655

MAD → SIN

2120	0715
2230	0830

SIN → HKT

0920	1005

HKT → SIN

1850	2135

SIN → KUL   **KUL → SIN**

every half hour from 0600 to 2000
flight time one hour

SIN → OSA

1100	1935
2355	0645

OSA → SIN

1010	1550
1200	1740

SIN → PEN

1020	1130
1910	2020

PEN → SIN

1015	1130
1925	2040

11 Using the phone

A 👥 Discuss these questions:

- What do you like about using the phone?
- What do you dislike about making phone calls?
- What can go wrong when using different kinds of phone: mobile phone, payphone, cordless phone?
- Is it easier to communicate face-to-face than over the phone? Why/Why not?

B1 👥 Look at these rules of behaviour for using the phone. Which do you think are the three most important points?

Rules for using the phone — some DOs and DON'Ts

1 Have all the DOCUMENTS you need to hand before you dial the number.

2 Speak CLEARLY so that the other person can understand you easily.

3 Always CONFIRM each point of information you are given. Don't pretend that you have understood when you haven't.

4 Speak in a POLITE and FRIENDLY voice — the client can't see what a nice person you are.

5 Behave in an EFFICIENT way, even if you're just taking a message.

6 Make NOTES during a call — don't rely on your memory. Read all the important details back to the client from your notes.

7 Let the other person FINISH what they want to say — don't interrupt them.

8 Send a FOLLOW-UP fax or letter to confirm any important details (especially prices and dates), so that you both have a written record of them.

2 🔊 You'll hear three telephone calls. Note down the rule that each person failed to observe.

1 The receptionist didn't follow rule number ....
2 The information officer didn't follow rule number ....
3 The restaurant manager didn't follow rule number ....

3 🔊 Now listen to three more calls.
What do the same members of staff do better this time?

C 1 👥👥👥 Note down some questions that a visitor who has never visited your country before might ask about your own city or region. Then discuss how you'd answer each question.

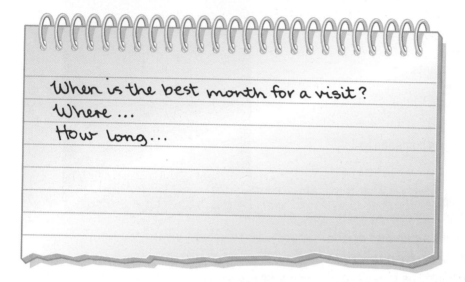

When is the best month for a visit?
Where ...
How long ...

2 Role play

👥👥👥 Student A plays the role of a VISITOR and Student B is an INFORMATION OFFICER in a tourist information office. Student C is the OBSERVER who will listen to the people on the phone and comment on how they sound. Did they follow all the Rules in B1? The two people on the phone should sit back-to-back, so that they can't see each other's faces and reactions.

3 The OBSERVER gives feedback to the speakers. Then change roles so that a different person has a turn at being the information officer.

4 The OBSERVER gives feedback to the speakers. Then change roles so that everyone has a turn at being the information officer.

> Good morning, Information office.
> Well, you can expect the best weather in . . .
> Certainly, yes, I can send you a list of all the hotels.
> You can get here by car or by train.
> The nearest airport is . . .
> Let me see, yes, it's 4th July.

> If you smile while you're talking on the phone, your listener can 'hear' your smile. But it's best not to try to be funny or make jokes over the phone — your listener may think you're being sarcastic, or may not share your sense of humour.

12 How may I help you?

A1 Listen to three phone calls and tick the boxes to show what each caller wants to know.

1 The first client wants to reserve a table for …
   lunch today. ☐
   dinner tonight. ☐
   lunch tomorrow. ☐

2 The second client wants to …
   cancel his booking. ☐
   change his booking. ☐
   confirm his booking. ☐

3 The third client wants someone to …
   repair a lamp. ☐
   replace a lamp. ☐
   bring an extra lamp. ☐

2 👥 Listen to the calls again and decide which receptionist deals with the client best. Give your reasons.

B1 👥 Complete this dialogue with your own ideas. Use some of the phrases in the speech balloon.

> Good morning, Royal Hotel, this is . . . speaking. How may I help you?
> Hello, . . ., how can I help you?
> Who's speaking, please?
> Hello, Reception. This is . . . speaking.
> Could you hold the line for a moment, please? I'll put you through to . . .
> Could you say that again, please?
> Could you spell that for me, please?
> Could I call you back later? . . . What's your number?

TRAVEL AGENT:	Hello, Transworld Travel, this is . . . speaking.
CLIENT:	Hello, my name's David Green.
TRAVEL AGENT:	.... ?
CLIENT:	Well, I bought a flight ticket from Frankfurt to Mexico City from you last week and now I need to change the outward flight date.
TRAVEL AGENT:	All right, I'll just get your file. .... ?
CLIENT:	All right.
TRAVEL AGENT:	Yes, here it is. .... ?
CLIENT:	Yes, the flight number is LH 414 and the date of travel is May 13th.

TRAVEL AGENT:	.... ?
CLIENT:	I want to depart on May 15th now by the same flight.
TRAVEL AGENT:	All right, Mr Green. ....
CLIENT:	I see. How long do you think it will take you to sort it out?
TRAVEL AGENT:	It may take a while. .... ?
CLIENT:	Yes, certainly. My number is 555 6789 — extension 449.
TRAVEL AGENT:	.... ?
CLIENT:	Yes, it's 555 6789 — extension 449.
TRAVEL AGENT:	.... ?
CLIENT:	No, it's four *four* nine. And can you call me back before 3 o'clock, please?
TRAVEL AGENT:	....
CLIENT:	Good. I'll hear from you soon, then. Thank you very much.
TRAVEL AGENT:	....
CLIENT:	Goodbye.

2 Pronunciation

Listen and compare your ideas with the model version of the dialogue. Then practise it in pairs, taking it in turns to play the roles of the CLIENT and the TRAVEL AGENT. Make sure you sound as polite as possible.

C Role play

Imagine that you are a MEMBER OF STAFF and a CLIENT talking on the phone. The member of staff must find out some personal information about the client and write it down on the form. Ask the client to repeat or spell out any details you don't catch. Then change roles so that you both get a turn at asking the questions.

FULL NAME:

ADDRESS:

PHONE NUMBER:

PASSPORT NUMBER:

VEHICLE REGISTRATION NUMBER:

13 Answering enquiries

A

You'll hear two phone calls to a rail information office. Listen and fill in the missing information in the timetable.

train type train number		TGV EC21	CIS 35	TGV EC23	IC 335	TGV EC29	IC 329	EN 213	EN 223	EN 215	EN 219	EN 217
Paris Lyon	d	0714		1218		1548		1930	2004	2007		2209
Lausanne	a	1106				1945		|	|	|	|	|
Lausanne	d		1113			1953		|	|	|	|	|
Milan Centrale	a		1417			2345		|	|	|	0604	
Venice Santa Lucia	a							|	0845	|	|	
Florence SMN	a							|		0938	|	
Rome Termini	a										1126	

B

You'll hear six more phone calls. Note down the information each caller is given.

1 The fax number is ....
2 The post code is ....
3 Dinner is served from .... to ....
4 The phone number is ....
5 The price of a double room is from .... to .... , depending on the facilities.
6 The phone number is .... and the fax number is ....

> Everyone finds it hard to understand numbers in a foreign language, and sometimes even in their own language. Bear this in mind when you're using English to say numbers to a client whose first language isn't English. When giving out numbers, say them slowly and clearly.

C1 Pronunciation

Practise these phone calls in pairs. Make sure that you sound helpful
and friendly and that you give the requested information very clearly.
Sit back-to-back, or avoid looking at each other during the calls.

Hello, New Zealand Lodge Association. How may I help you?
— Could you tell me the phone number of Kingfish Lodge, please?
Yes, certainly. It's 64 9 405 0164.
— 64 9 405 0164?
Yes, that's right.
— Good. OK, thank you very much.
You're welcome.

Hello, New Zealand Lodge Association. How may I help you?
— Could you tell me the address of Inverness Estate, please?
Yes, certainly. It's Ness Valley Road, RD 5, Papakura, New Zealand.
— How do you spell that?
N E double S, Ness Valley Road, RD 5, PAPAKURA.
— Ness Valley Road, RD 5, PAPAKURA?
Yes, that's right.
— Good. Thank you very much.
You're welcome.

2 Role play

One of you should look at
Activity 8 on page 111, the other at
Activity 23 on page 119.

You'll be playing the roles of Tourist
and Information officer. Sit back-to-
back, or avoid looking at each other
during the calls. This role play is in
two parts.

> *I'm sorry, could you say
> that again, please?*
> *I'm sorry, could you say that
> again more slowly, please?*
> *Could you spell that for me,
> please?*

> *Yes, certainly. It's . . .*
> *I'll just check it for you. Just a
> moment, please.*
> *Could you hold the line for a
> moment, please? I'll just find out.*
> *Could I call you back with that
> information? . . . What's your
> number, please?*

A You'll hear a client leaving a message about some tickets you have been asked to deal with. Listen and decide what important information is missing from these notes. Now listen for a second time. What is noted down incorrectly?

> When taking a message, always check with the client that you have noted down the main points correctly — especially the names, dates, times, prices and numbers.

Horizon Travel

Date: 7 July   Time: 12.45

Message for: Gemma

From: Mr Boyle   Tel. No.: 324 9856

Mr Boyle wants to change his booking to New York with Atlantic Hols.
Now wants to fly on 16 Oct at 14:00, instead of 2 Oct. Prefers Metro
Hotel to Rotterdam Hotel.
Return flight can be 09.30 or 22.25.
Call him on Friday.

B1 You'll hear two messages which have been left on answer machines. Note down the main points of each message on the message pads.

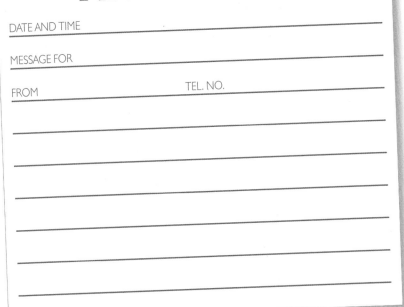

~ PHOENIX HOTEL ~

DATE AND TIME

MESSAGE FOR

FROM   TEL. NO.

Newtown-on-sea
INFORMATION BUREAU

Date and time

Message for

From

Tel. No.

2 👥 Compare your notes and discuss these questions:

- Did you miss any important information?
- Did you include any unnecessary information?
- Is your handwriting readable and could another person understand the message?

3 Writing

Rewrite the messages in note form so that another person can understand them clearly.

C Role play

💬 👥 One of you should look at Activity 9 on page 112, the other at Activity 24 on page 120.

You'll be giving and receiving some more messages. Note down the information you're given on the message pads. This role play is in four parts.

BAY VIEW
H O T E L

Date and time:

Message for:

From:

Tel:

_____

BAY VIEW
H O T E L

Date and time:

Message for:

From:

Tel:

Making notes involves choosing the important information to write down. You can't write down every word the client says, so you have to decide what is relevant and what is irrelevant.

A 👤👤👤👤 **Discuss these questions:**

- What is usually served for breakfast in a hotel in your country?
- What do people in your country usually have for breakfast when they're at *home*?
- What do *you* usually have for breakfast?

BREAKFAST

Kindly indicate the number of orders and the time you wish breakfast to be served. Please hang this menu on the outside doorknob before 11:00 P.M.

Date	Room No.	Name	No. of Persons

To be served between:
- ❑ 6:30 ~ 7:00
- ❑ 7:00 ~ 7:30
- ❑ 7:30 ~ 8:00
- ❑ 8:00 ~ 8:30
- ❑ 8:30 ~ 9:00
- ❑ 9:00 ~ 9:30
- ❑ 9:30 ~ 10:00

AMERICAN BREAKFAST ¥2,000	Orders

Juice   ❑ Orange   ❑ Tomato   ❑ Grapefruit
Eggs   ❑ Fried
　　　❑ Scrambled
　　　❑ Poached   with ❑ Ham ❑ Bacon ❑ Sausage
　　　❑ Boiled ❑ Minutes
Breakfast Rolls with Jam & Marmalade
Beverage   ❑ Coffee
　　　❑ Tea   with ❑ Milk ❑ Lemon
　　　❑ Milk

B You'll hear three guests phoning to order breakfast in their rooms. Listen and note down (1) what the guest in Room 213 wants by ticking the breakfast menu; (2) what the guests in Rooms 121 and 305 want by filling in the form.

Orders

CONTINENTAL BREAKFAST   ¥1,100

Juice   ❏ Orange   ❏ Tomato   ❏ Grapefruit
Breakfast Rolls with Jam & Marmalade
Beverage   ❏ Coffee
              ❏ Tea   with ❏ Milk ❏ Lemon
              ❏ Milk

The items on the regular Room Service breakfast menu are also available. Please write in here any you would like.

❏
❏
❏

A 10% service charge,
3% consumption tax and
3% meals and hotel tax
will be added to the
above prices.

Holiday Inn
Metropolitan Tokyo

ROOM NUMBER	TIME REQUIRED	BREAKFAST ORDER
121		
305		

C 1 Pronunciation

Listen, and repeat the questions used by the person taking the order.

I'd like some tea, please.
— Would you like it with milk or lemon?
Can I have some fruit juice, please?
— Would you like orange juice or grapefruit juice?

2 Role play

👥 Take it in turns to play the roles of a GUEST and a WAITER/WAITRESS.

GUEST	WAITER/WAITRESS (*try to sound bright and helpful*)
bacon and eggs	scrambled or fried?
an egg	poached or boiled?
tea	with milk or lemon?
fruit juice	orange or grapefruit?
hot drink	tea or coffee?
coffee	with cream or without?
fried eggs	with ham or bacon?
breakfast rolls	butter or margarine?

D Role play

👥 Take it in turns to play the roles of a GUEST ordering breakfast over the phone, and a MEMBER OF STAFF taking the order. Order from the same breakfast menu that you used before.

A1 You'll hear a description of how to make the Spanish dish, *paella*. Before you listen, look at the picture. How many of the ingredients can you identify? Do you know what goes into a *paella*?

2 Listen to the description and decide if these statements are true (✓) or false (✗).

The rice is cooked first. ☐

The basic ingredients are stir-fried. ☐

A *paella* is baked in the oven. ☐

It must be stirred all the time it's cooking. ☐

The rice takes about 20 minutes to cook. ☐

3 👥 Discuss these questions:

- Is it a dish you'd like to eat? Why/Why not?
- Is it a dish you'd like to make? Why/Why not?

B1 👥👥 Look at the pictures. Use the words in the list below to identify the methods of cooking shown in each one. One method isn't illustrated. Which one is it?

steam	boil	grill/broil	stir-fry
deep fry	bake	roast	

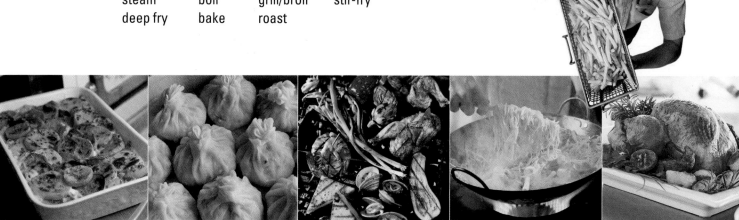

lemon sorbet

risotto

2 👥 **How do things taste? Discuss how you think these dishes taste, using the words in the list.**

> spicy (hot)   creamy (rich)
> plain   sweet   salty
> sour   bitter

chocolate mousse

curry

bread

3 👥👥 Think of some more ingredients, dishes or sauces that you can describe with the words in the list above.

C1 Think about dishes you know — starters, main courses and desserts.
How can you describe them to a guest?
Write a short menu including five dishes that are typical of your country.

2   Role play

👥 Take it in turns to play the roles of a CUSTOMER and a WAITER/WAITRESS.

WAITER/WAITRESS
  Show your menu to the customer.
CUSTOMER
  Ask about each of the dishes on the menu.
WAITER/WAITRESS
  Explain how each dish is prepared.

> *Moules marinière?*
>
> *Lasagne al forno?*
>
> *Paella a la valenciana?*

> *That's mussels cooked in wine with onions and herbs.*
> *That's layers of pasta, meat sauce and creamy sauce baked in the oven.*
> *That's rice cooked with meat, shellfish and vegetables flavoured with saffron.*

17 May I take your order?

A1 👥 Note down three questions a customer might ask about this menu. Decide how you would answer each question.

2 🔊 You'll hear three guests ordering from the menu. Note down their orders, including the *changes* they request.

3 👥 🔊 Listen again and then discuss these questions:

- Which waiter or waitress did the best job?
- Who made a mistake? What was the mistake?
- Who was the most polite?
  Who was the most efficient?
  Who was the most friendly?

MENU

Appetizers and soups
Soup of the day
Cream of asparagus soup
Melon with port wine
Six oysters
Grilled sardines with lemon juice and garlic
Smoked salmon
Waldorf salad

Entrées
Grilled fillet steak served with French fries
Pan-fried trout served with tagliatelle
Venison steak with pepper sauce served
with roast potatoes
Veal schnitzel served with new potatoes
Grilled lamb chops served with sauté potatoes

All served with vegetables of the day

Today's specials
Tomato, spinach and eggplant casserole
Poached salmon with a ginger and lime juice sauce

B1 Fill the blanks in this dialogue.

WAITER: Are you ready to order, sir?

CUSTOMER: Yes. I'd like a steak, please.

WAITER: Certainly. How ....?

CUSTOMER: Medium rare, please. And can I have it with rice instead of French fries?

WAITER: Yes, of course. Would .... ?

CUSTOMER: Yes, a mixed salad would be nice.

WAITER:	Fine, sir, and would .... ?
CUSTOMER:	Oh, yes. Let's see … What's the soup of the day?
WAITER:	Today we have cream of asparagus — it's made with fresh asparagus.
CUSTOMER:	Good. OK, I'll have that.
WAITER:	And would .... ?
CUSTOMER:	No, I'll have a beer, I think. Do you have local draught beer?
WAITER:	No, I'm afraid not. Would .... ?
CUSTOMER:	Yes, OK, never mind. That'll be fine.
WAITER:	So, that's a medium rare steak with rice and a mixed salad. And cream of asparagus soup to start with. Is that right?
CUSTOMER:	Yes, that's right. And can I have some bread, please?
WAITER:	....
CUSTOMER:	Thanks very much.

"One medium rare and one with honey."

2 Pronunciation

🔊 **Listen to a model version of the dialogue. Then practise it in pairs, taking it in turns to play the roles of the WAITER/WAITRESS and the CUSTOMER. Make sure you sound as friendly and helpful as possible.**

C1 👥 Add one more item to each part of the menu, including another special.

2 Role play

👥👥 Take it in turns to play the roles of a WAITER/WAITRESS and a table of two or three CUSTOMERS . Use the menu opposite.

After each turn, the guests give feedback on how well the waiter or waitress did their job.

3 👥 What are the local specialities of your region? What would you say to a customer, to encourage him or her to try them? How are they prepared?

> When taking an order, or making notes on what a client tells you, always double-check that you've noted things down right. This also gives the clients a chance to make sure they haven't made any mistakes. And to change their mind if they want to.

> *Are you ready to order?*
> *Would you like an appetizer?*
> *And to follow . . . ?*
> *I'm sure you'll enjoy that — it's delicious.*
> *May I recommend the . . .? It's one of the chef's specialities.*
> *. . . is a local speciality, I can recommend it.*
> *And what would you like to drink?*
> *So that's . . . [and check you've noted everything down correctly] — is that right?*
> *So that's one . . . , one . . . and two . . . — is that right?*
> *Enjoy your meal!*

18 Drinks, snacks and desserts

A 👥 Look at the pictures and label the drinks that are shown. Then discuss these questions:

● Which of the drinks are the most popular in your country?
● Which very popular drinks are *not* shown?

B 👥 Match these words to the drinks below. Some of them have two or more matches — try to find them all.

a   glass bottle carafe carton can jar jug pot cup
of   beer wine milk tea lemonade orange juice honey

EXAMPLES: *A glass of beer*
             A bottle of beer
             A can of beer

C1 👥 Look at the menu opposite and add suitable prices. Then add one more item (including price) to each section of the menu.

What questions would a customer ask about the items on the menu? How would you answer their questions?

2 Role play

👥👥 Take it in turns to play the roles of a WAITER/WAITRESS and some CUSTOMERS at the Palm Beach Café.

CUSTOMERS   Order something to eat and something to drink. Then imagine time has passed and ask for your bill and pay it.

WAITER/WAITRESS   Take the order. Then imagine time has passed and present the bill.

> What would you like to drink?
> Would you like something to eat as well
> So that's . . . [and check you've understood the order correctly] — is that right?
> Did you enjoy your . . . ?
> That comes to 43 dollars altogether.
> And that's 7 dollars in change.
> Thank you very much.

PALM BEACH café

Price

Snacks
Home-made hamburger with french fries and salad
Freshly made sandwiches with a choice of fillings
Waldorf salad
Our special Club sandwich

Desserts and cakes
Chocolate mousse
Profiteroles with chocolate sauce
Fresh fruit salad
Apple pie with whipped cream
Carrot cake
Black Forest cherry cake

Drinks
Espresso, cappuccino or filter coffee
Indian, China or green tea
Iced tea or coffee
Freshly squeezed orange or grapefruit juice
Thick chocolate, vanilla or strawberry ice cream milkshake
Home-made lemonade

Enjoy your meal !

D 1 You'll hear three people talking about their work. Listen to what they say about what they do and what they enjoy ✓ and don't enjoy X about their work.

Helen
wine
waitress

Fiona
barmaid

Sam
restaurant
manager

✓ or X

alcohol makes 20% of people behave badly ☐
asking noisy customers to be quiet ☐
being busy ☐
dealing with complaints ☐
explaining what things are ☐
hard work, late nights, long shifts ☐
large orders cause delays for other tables ☐
meeting people from other countries ☐
not being too close to the customers ☐
recommending drinks ☐

2 Discuss these questions:

● What do you think is the worst thing about each person's job?
● What do you think is the best thing?

19 Eating habits

A1 Read each of these newspaper articles and then write down your answers to the questions below.

1

Greek villagers live longer

A report published today in the British Medical Journal claims that a Mediterranean diet will help you to live longer. Greek researchers have found that people who eat plenty of fruit, vegetables and olive oil, and low quantities of meat and dairy products will live to a healthy old age.

Ten years ago the researchers measured the food intake of 182 men and women aged over 70 in three Greek villages. This year they returned to look at the numbers who had died. They found that the villagers who ate a traditional diet had a 17 per cent reduction in the chance of death compared to those who did not.

The traditional Mediterranean diet consists of a high consumption of olive oil, beans, cereals, vegetables and fruits, a low consumption of dairy products and meat – and a moderate consumption of alcohol.

Mediterranean diet is the way to eat and drink your way to health

MORE evidence that Mediterranean food and drink are good for the health has emerged in three studies published today.

They show that wine is better than beer or spirits at protecting against heart disease, that olive oil can prevent bowel cancer and that garlic lowers cholesterol levels.

One study found that wine drinkers are less likely to die from heart disease and cancer than people who prefer spirits or beer. A long-term study into 24,000 Danes showed that even heavy drinkers are less at risk if wine is their preferred drink.

Another study weighed up the evidence for garlic and cholesterol. It found that garlic lowers levels of harmful cholesterol, but that the evidence may not be as clear-cut as some garlic-lovers claim.

The third study looked at food preferences and bowel cancer in 28 countries, including Britain, the United States, Brazil and China. More than three quarters of the difference in rates of bowel cancer was explained by just three dietary factors. Meat and fish increased the risk, but a diet high in olive oil reduced it.

3

Atkins diet 'a gamble'

Followers of the Atkins diet are gambling with their future health, according to a top nutrition expert

Dr Susan Jebb, from the Medical Research Council's Human Nutrition Research Centre in Cambridge, said it would be "negligent" to recommend the diet to anyone overweight.

She said the claims made for the Atkins diet were based on "pseudo-science".

She argued that despite a number of small studies, no one knew what the long-term effects of the Atkins diet might be.

But data gained from large diet investigations involving thousands of participants had set alarm bells ringing.

The Atkins diet cuts out carbohydrates and boosts consumption of protein without having to avoid fatty foods.

It is a favourite of celebrities such as Jennifer Aniston, Renee Zellweger and Minnie Driver.

Dr Robert Atkins, who developed the diet, believed that carbohydrates such as bread, pasta, rice and starchy veg-

etables over-stimulated the production of insulin, resulting in hunger and weight gain.

But Dr Jebb said the diet was a leap in the dark because it meant such a dramatic change in eating habits.

For most people, protein accounts for a mere 15 per cent of the calorie intake. But much higher levels are consumed by people following the Atkins diet.

Dr Jebb's warning comes two months after two teams of American scientists declared that the Atkins diet was effective and safe.

The two studies, published in the New England Journal of Medicine, found that the diet resulted in more weight loss than conventional low-fat diets.

But Dr Jebb said these studies and others focusing on the Atkins diet were too small, short and limited to provide any meaningful evidence.

---

1 According to the first article, what is the effect of the Mediterranean diet?

2 According to the second article, what are three healthy parts of the Mediterranean diet?

3 According to the third article, why is the Atkins diet 'a gamble'?

2 👤👤👤👤 Discuss these questions:

- Do you follow the Mediterranean diet? Why/Why not?
- Have you ever tried to lose weight? What did you eat and what didn't you eat?

B1 You'll hear four people talking about what they eat. Listen and put a tick (✓) by the things they do eat and a cross (✗) by the things that they don't eat.

Sally   beef   cheese   chicken   dairy products   eggs   nuts   pulses   vegetables

Tim   cheese   commercial meat products   free range meat   garlic   pasta   spicy foods   vegetables

Peter   bread   cakes   eggs   fish   meat   pasta   vegetables   wheat flour

Steve   chicken   chocolate   convenience foods   desserts   fish   nuts

2 👥 Look again at the menu on page 40. What would you recommend from the menu to each of the speakers?

C1 👥👥 Carry out this survey with the members of your group. Fill in each box with the number of times that each person tells you. First of all, fill in your own answers.

Survey on eating habits

How many times have you eaten each of these kinds of food or meal during the past seven days?

☐ ☐ ☐ ☐ ☐   wholemeal bread   white bread ☐ ☐ ☐ ☐ ☐

☐ ☐ ☐ ☐ ☐   fast food   a traditional local meal ☐ ☐ ☐ ☐ ☐

☐ ☐ ☐ ☐ ☐   a meal with meat   a vegetarian meal ☐ ☐ ☐ ☐ ☐

☐ ☐ ☐ ☐ ☐   convenience food   food prepared from fresh ingredients ☐ ☐ ☐ ☐ ☐

☐ ☐ ☐ ☐ ☐   a snack or a sandwich   a full meal ☐ ☐ ☐ ☐ ☐

☐ ☐ ☐ ☐ ☐   a meal in a cafeteria   a meal in a restaurant ☐ ☐ ☐ ☐ ☐

☐ ☐ ☐ ☐ ☐   a meal at home   a picnic ☐ ☐ ☐ ☐ ☐

2 Compare the results of your survey with the other groups and discuss these questions:

- Which are the *three* most popular kinds of food or meal in your group? (Which scored the highest in your survey?)
- Which are the three *least* popular? (Which scored the lowest in the survey?)
- Why do so many people eat junk food when they know it isn't healthy?

20 Welcome to our restaurant!

A1 Find the answers to these questions in the leaflet opposite:

1 Two things are not modern at Chez Fred. What are they?
2 What is modern about the restaurant?
3 How many people does the restaurant seat?
4 Can you buy a meal at Chez Fred to take home to eat?
5 What can you buy at Chez Fred apart from fish and chips?
6 In the old days, how were fish and chips wrapped?

2 🕴🕴 Discuss these questions:

● If Mr Capel opened a branch of Chez Fred in your town or city, how successful would it be? Why?
● If you could open your own restaurant or café:
  What kind of place would it be?
  What kinds of food and drink would you serve?

B Grammar *Did you do it?/Have you done it?*

Here are just a few things that have to be done before opening a restaurant for business:

lay the tables	photocopy the menus
clean the floor	buy flowers for the tables
put the drinks in the fridge	prepare the reserved tables
unlock the door	put today's menu in the showcase outside

🕴🕴 Take it in turns to ask each other if the other things on the list have been done. Follow this pattern:

Ask: *Have you laid the tables?*
Reply: — *Yes, I have. I laid them an hour ago.*   or   — *Oh, dear. I forgot to lay them. I'll do it now.*

C 🕴🕴🕴🕴 Imagine that you're setting up your own restaurant — a place that's friendly and welcoming, and not too elegant or too expensive.

1 Plan a menu for your restaurant. Include one typical national dish and one regional speciality.

A set meal (*table d'hôte*), rather than a long *à la carte* menu is probably simplest. Don't worry about prices — all meals are on the house for the opening night !
What will you call your restaurant? Decide on a good name for it.

2 Role play

One team invites the members of another team (who are English-speaking guests) to come to the opening night of their restaurant. They welcome their guests, show them to their 'tables' and take their orders.

3 *Change roles* Now the members of the first team are the guests at the other team's restaurant.

4 Writing

Write a short newspaper report (about 50 words) describing the opening night.

The Capel family, well known locally for producing the finest Fish & Chips, are proud to announce the opening of their new venture "Chez Fred".

Our new Westbourne premises (formerly known as The Buccaneer), have undergone a complete refit in the style of the Edwardian age of the early 1900s.

The result is a new attractive licensed restaurant catering for **50** persons together with an outstanding quick service takeaway section, both of which are serviced by the most up to date frying equipment modern technology can provide.

Fred Capel, widely acknowledged within the trade as one of Britain's most accomplished fish and chip fryers, heads the professional team at Chez Fred, and their common aim is to provide a service second to none at value-for-money prices.

Our products are superb – we assure you, our reputation guarantees it! Beautifully prepared and cooked fish, cocooned in our specially formulated crisp batter, together with chips like mother makes, provide an unbeatable combination! *A taste of long ago, in fact.*

In addition to our scrumptious fish menu, we also produce mouth-watering Southern Fried Chicken. Good size portions of fresh chicken coated with our special breading and pressure-fried to perfection, a delicious alternative for those non-fish eaters.

Our exciting restaurant menu will include an imaginative selection of desserts, plus regular "Specials" — all designed to tempt you, so visit us soon. We think you'll agree — *Fish & Chips have come a long way since the newspaper wrapping days!*

Superb fish & chips

A1 Look at the phone message and the email and the letter responding to it. The letter and the email both contain two mistakes. What are they?

MESSAGE FROM:
Mr Robert Harris of Chimera SA

DATE AND TIME:
11 June   12.45

Mr Harris wants to reserve a private room for a party of ten for Sunday 23rd June at 20.30. Can we do a special 4-course menu? The meal is to welcome a group of foreign visitors who want to eat local specialities. Please quote price including wine.

Magnolia
R E S T A U R A N T

Mr Robert Harris
Chimera SA
100 Liberty Boulevard
Freetown

11 June [year]

Dear Mr Harris,

Thank you very much for your enquiry. I am happy to say that we can reserve a private room for you for the evening of June 23 from 8pm.

Our chef has prepared a sample menu for you, which is enclosed. As you can see, he has included several typical dishes from our region. I feel sure you will find this suitable for your guests. Two very good local wines have been included on the menu.

For a party of ten people our price per person would be $45, including 15% service. Wine will be charged extra.

I look forward to hearing from you. If you have any questions about the menu or any further suggestions, please call me.

I would be grateful if you could confirm this booking in writing by the end of this month.

Thank you very much for your interest in our restaurant. We look forward to welcoming you and your party.

Yours sincerely,

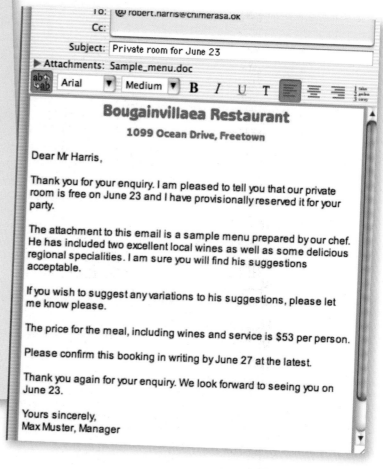

TO: robert.narris@chimerasa.ok

Cc:

Subject: Private room for June 23

Attachments: Sample_menu.doc

Arial   Medium   **B** *I* U T

Bougainvillaea Restaurant
1099 Ocean Drive, Freetown

Dear Mr Harris,

Thank you for your enquiry. I am pleased to tell you that our private room is free on June 23 and I have provisionally reserved it for your party.

The attachment to this email is a sample menu prepared by our chef. He has included two excellent local wines as well as some delicious regional specialities. I am sure you will find his suggestions acceptable.

If you wish to suggest any variations to his suggestions, please let me know please.

The price for the meal, including wines and service is $53 per person.

Please confirm this booking in writing by June 27 at the latest.

Thank you again for your enquiry. We look forward to seeing you on June 23.

Yours sincerely,
Max Muster, Manager

2 👥 Discuss these questions:

● What is the main difference between the email and the letter?
● Which would the client prefer to receive? Why?

We usually use more words to say something than we do to write it. But writing takes much longer than a conversation because of the time it takes to prepare, write and edit.

B 👥 Rearrange the eleven parts of this letter to give the correct layout.

1. Thank you very much for your letter.

2. Dear Mrs Spencer,

3. Yours sincerely,

4. The price per night is $120 including evening meal and breakfast.

5. Please let us know if you intend to arrive after 6pm.

6. # Royal Zenda Hotel
   115–121 Constitution Avenue, Hentzau, R-10034, Ruritania

7. Ms Dorothy Spencer
   123 Pine Avenue
   Newtown NN3 9DN
   Great Britain

8. *Rupert Meyer*
   Rupert Meyer
   Reservations Manager

9. We look forward to welcoming you on Sunday, December 4.

10. I am happy to confirm your booking for the nights of 4 December to 9 December. We have reserved a double room on the second floor, with bathroom, balcony and sea view.

11. 4 July [year]

C1 🔊 Imagine that you're working at your local tourist information office. You'll hear a telephone enquiry recorded on the answer machine. Listen and note down the caller's name and fax number and the information the caller requires.

MESSAGE FROM

2 Writing

Reply to the message by fax or email, giving the requested information about your town or city.

A fax or email can be written in a less formal style than a letter. People don't expect a fax or email to look as good as a letter, but a good-looking communication of any kind gives a better impression than a messy one.

22 Confirming reservations

A1 Look at these two letters. Which of them would you prefer to receive? Why?

BELLEVUE H·O·T·E·L

22 April [year]

Henry Beaumont
144 Riverside Drive
Springfield

Dear Mr Beaumont,

Thank you very much for your telephone call. I am writing to you now to confirm your reservation for two adjoining double rooms with bath for the nights of July 14 to 23. Both rooms have a sea view and are on the fourth floor of the hotel.

The cost for half board (modified American plan) is $85 per person per night, including taxes and service.

I enclose two brochures describing our hotel and its facilities. If you have any questions, we shall be pleased to answer them.

Please let us know if you are arriving at the hotel later than 7pm.

We look forward to welcoming you to the Bellevue on July 14. We hope you will enjoy your stay with us.

Yours sincerely,

Homeleigh Hotel

22 April [year]

Mrs Rita Potter
123 Oakdale Road
Shelbyville

Dear Mrs Potter,

I am sending you this letter to confirm your telephone booking for two double rooms here from July 14 to 24 (10 nights). The two rooms are on the third floor. There is a connecting door and the rooms have balconies with sea views.

The price of the accommodation is $90 per person per night for demi pension (half board). This includes taxes and service.

In case you are interested, I enclose a brochure about the hotel. This tells you all you need to know about the hotel and what it has to offer.

You must let me know if you plan to arrive at the hotel after 7 o'clock.

Yours sincerely,

2 Highlight four phrases in your preferred letter which help to make it seem better.

B1 You'll hear a phone call in which a client is booking a conference room at a hotel. Listen and fill in the missing information on the booking form opposite. Tick (✓) the boxes to show which services and equipment she asks for.

2 Draft a letter to Jane Barratt confirming the reservation.

3 Show each other your letters. What are the best things in each letter?

4 Writing

Write a final improved draft of the letter, using the best ideas from each letter.

Useful phrases

If you have any further questions, please let us know and we shall be delighted to help.

Thank you for choosing our hotel.

Please let us know if you have any special requests.

ROYAL SUITE CONFERENCE ROOM BOOKING

CLIENT'S NAME	*Jane Barratt*
COMPANY NAME	
COMPANY ADDRESS	
PHONE	FAX
TOTAL NUMBER OF PARTICIPANTS	
Date	
Starting time	
Coffee break from	to
Lunch break from	to
Finishing time	

CATERING

coffee	☐	sandwiches	☐
tea	☐	buffet lunch	☐
pastries	☐	sit-down lunch	☐

EQUIPMENT

overhead projector	☐	cassette player	☐
VCR	☐	microphone	☐
TV	☐	data projector	☐

Some "GOLDEN RULES" for writing letters and emails

- Decide what to say before you start to write. If you don't, the sentences are likely to go on and on and on until you can think of a good way to finish. In other words, make sure that you plan ahead.

- Put each separate idea in a separate paragraph.

- Use short sentences.

- Use short words that everyone can understand. You may be writing to people whose English isn't as good as yours.

- Think about your reader. Your letters and emails should be…

  Clear – make sure the reader knows exactly what you mean.

  Complete – make sure you give the reader all the necessary information.

  Courteous – write in a sincere, polite tone.

  Correct – the reader may be confused if there are too many mistakes in grammar, punctuation or spelling.

- Check your letter through before you print it – and correct any mistakes you find.

> When writing to a woman, make sure you use her preferred style of address: Mrs, Miss or Ms. If in doubt, use Ms.

A1 Look at these emails. Find the mistakes in each one.

2 Writing

Choose one of the emails and rewrite it correctly.

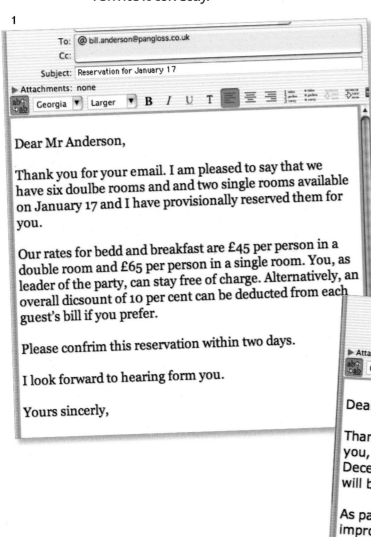

1

To: @ bill.anderson@pangloss.co.uk
Cc:
Subject: Reservation for January 17
Attachments: none

Georgia | Larger | B I U T

Dear Mr Anderson,

Thank you for your email. I am pleased to say that we have six doulbe rooms and and two single rooms available on January 17 and I have provisionally reserved them for you.

Our rates for bedd and breakfast are £45 per person in a double room and £65 per person in a single room. You, as leader of the party, can stay free of charge. Alternatively, an overall dicsount of 10 per cent can be deducted from each guest's bill if you prefer.

Please confrim this reservation within two days.

I look forward to hearing form you.

Yours sincerly,

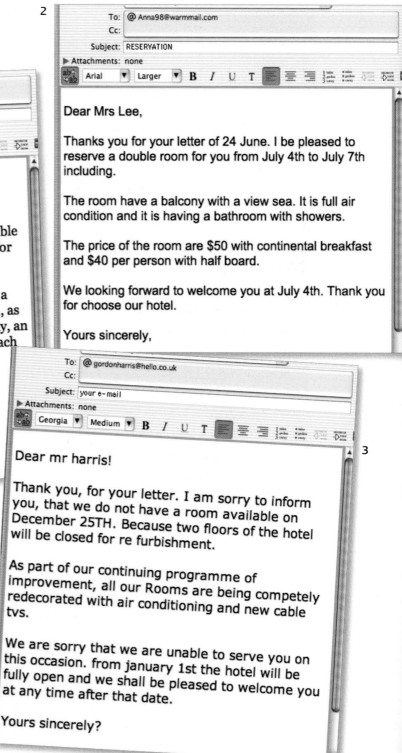

2

To: @ Anna98@warmmail.com
Cc:
Subject: RESERVATION
Attachments: none

Arial | Larger | B I U T

Dear Mrs Lee,

Thanks you for your letter of 24 June. I be pleased to reserve a double room for you from July 4th to July 7th including.

The room have a balcony with a view sea. It is full air condition and it is having a bathroom with showers.

The price of the room are $50 with continental breakfast and $40 per person with half board.

We looking forward to welcome you at July 4th. Thank you for choose our hotel.

Yours sincerely,

3

To: @ gordonharris@hello.co.uk
Cc:
Subject: your e-mail
Attachments: none

Georgia | Medium | B I U T

Dear mr harris!

Thank you, for your letter. I am sorry to inform you, that we do not have a room available on December 25TH. Because two floors of the hotel will be closed for re furbishment.

As part of our continuing programme of improvement, all our Rooms are being competely redecorated with air conditioning and new cable tvs.

We are sorry that we are unable to serve you on this occasion. from january 1st the hotel will be fully open and we shall be pleased to welcome you at any time after that date.

Yours sincerely?

If you send someone a letter or email, make sure it gives the right impression. Unclear layout or untidy presentation may suggest that you are inefficient or don't care.

B1 👥 Imagine that you work at the Seaview Hotel. Decide together how to reply to this letter. (The chambermaid found the iron and the address book, but not the Walkman; you tried to phone Ms Duckworth but there was no reply.)

Make notes of the information you'll give in your reply.

2 Writing

Write a letter responding to Ms Duckworth.

3 👥 Read each other's letters and look for any mistakes your partner has made in:

spelling   punctuation   grammar

Correct the mistakes that your partner points out to you.

4 *Join a different partner* Read each other's letters. If you were a client, which of them would you prefer to receive? Why?

---

430 Albany Avenue
West Fleet
Surrey WT9 4PJ

Seaview Hotel
100 East Cliff Drive
Budmouth
Dorset DT34 7JT
Phone/Fax: 01254 776667

14 August [year]

Dear Sir or Madam,

I have just returned from a business trip, during which I spent the night of 3 August at your hotel. When I unpacked my suitcase I discovered that several things were missing: a portable iron, my address book and a Walkman. I stayed in several different hotels during the trip but yours was the only one where I had to leave in a hurry because I did not receive a wake-up call. This is why I am fairly sure that I left all these things at your hotel.

Please let me know if you have found these items. If you would be kind enough to send them to me, I will be happy to send you a cheque for the postage.

Yours sincerely,

Susan Duckworth

S. Duckworth

Before you print out a letter or email, always check it through to make sure that you have included all the necessary information — and that you haven't made any mistakes in numbers, prices or dates.

24 We are very sorry ...

A

You'll hear two people talking about dealing with a letter of complaint from a client. Listen and decide if these statements are true (✓) or false (✗).

1 Janine's clients complained because ...
   they had to pay twice for their accommodation. ☐   their hotel room was double booked. ☐

2 She is going to write to apologise. ☐   A face-to-face apology is enough in this case. ☐

3 Robert's guest complained because ...
   she was woken by the fire alarm in the night. ☐   her room was cold and the water was cold. ☐

4 He is going to explain that it wasn't his fault. ☐   He is going to write a letter of apology. ☐

B1

Look at this extract from an email from Mr Cross, a client, and then read the two replies below.

Which reply would you prefer to receive if you were the client? Why? (If neither reply seems satisfactory, why not?)

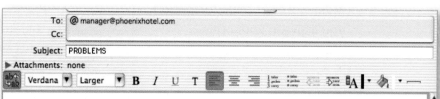

> To: @ manager@phoenixhotel.com
> Cc:
> Subject: PROBLEMS
> Attachments: none
>
> Verdana ▼ Larger ▼ **B** *I* U T
>
> The fire alarm went off in the middle of the night and we followed the indicated escape route. But the back stairs were blocked with boxes and we had to go back to the main stairs. In a real emergency this would have been very dangerous.
>
> We all had to stand in the street which was cold and dark. The hotel staff did not seem to know what had happened. We were allowed back in after about an hour. Only later did we find out (from another guest) that there had been a minor fire in the boiler room.
>
> There was no heating the next day because of the boiler fault. We asked the housekeeper for extra blankets but none came.
>
> The next morning we complained about the blocked fire stairs at the front desk and they apologised, but in the evening the boxes were still there.

1

> To: @ cross@seeingred.co.uk
> Cc:
> Subject: Your email
> Attachments: none
>
> Courier ▼ Larger ▼ **B** *I* U T
>
> Dear Mr Cross,
>
> Thank you for your email of 3 November. I am very sorry that there were problems during your stay with us in October. It will take me a few days to look into this matter because I need to talk to all the members of staff who were involved. I will telephone you as soon as I can with my response.
>
> I would like you to know that we are taking your complaint very seriously. You are a valued guest. If you are dissatisfied with our service this gives us a chance to make any improvements necessary.
>
> I will contact you if I need to know more from you to help me resolve this matter. Thank you for being so patient.
>
> Yours sincerely,

2

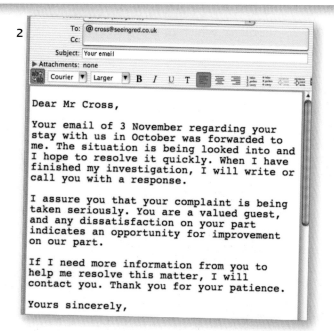

> To: @ cross@seeingred.co.uk
> Cc:
> Subject: Your email
> Attachments: none
>
> Courier ▼ Larger ▼ **B** *I* U T
>
> Dear Mr Cross,
>
> Your email of 3 November regarding your stay with us in October was forwarded to me. The situation is being looked into and I hope to resolve it quickly. When I have finished my investigation, I will write or call you with a response.
>
> I assure you that your complaint is being taken seriously. You are a valued guest, and any dissatisfaction on your part indicates an opportunity for improvement on our part.
>
> If I need more information from you to help me resolve this matter, I will contact you. Thank you for your patience.
>
> Yours sincerely,

2  Imagine that you are the hotel manager. After investigating the situation, you have now found out that all the client's complaints are justified. Decide what you are going to do to deal with the situation.

3 Look at the letters in Activity 38 on page 126. Highlight the useful phrases in the letter of apology which you can use in your letter to Mr Cross.

4 Writing

Write a letter to Mr Cross explaining what action you've taken.

C Writing

Imagine that you're the travel agent who recommended the Inferno Hotel to Mr and Mrs Wild. Write a reply to this letter from them.

> We are writing to you to complain about the Inferno Hotel, which you recommended to us and booked for us. We have just returned from our holiday and we did not enjoy ourselves.
>
> We booked a family room for three people (there are two of us, and our son Kevin, aged 16). We were given a small, dark room on the top floor with a double bed and an uncomfortable camp bed, which partly blocked the door to the bathroom.
>
> We were promised a sea view, but our room overlooked the back yard and you could only see the sea if you leant out of the window. Because of the cooking smells from the kitchen, we had to keep our windows closed. The air conditioning was so noisy that we couldn't sleep unless we turned it off at night.
>
> We complained to the management about our room, but the hotel was completely full and no other rooms were available. The staff were very apologetic but there was nothing they could do.
>
> Another problem was that the food was disappointing. The portions were enormous but the dishes on the daily menu were monotonous and tasteless. The head waiter advised us to order à la carte if we wanted better food, but this would have been expensive.
>
> The swimming pool was not cleaned once during our week there. The water became dirty with more and more leaves sinking to the bottom. There was an extra charge for the use of sunbeds, which seemed unreasonable to us, but the alternative was lying on the concrete.
>
> It made things worse when we found out in conversation with other guests that everyone we talked to had paid less than we had. One couple who had made a last-minute booking had paid half what we had for a similar room!
>
> Yours sincerely,
>
> *Edna Wild* Nigel Wild

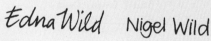

A1 Read these emails and look at the room chart of the Royal Hotel below. There is one mistake in the way the room chart has been filled out. Find the mistake and correct it.

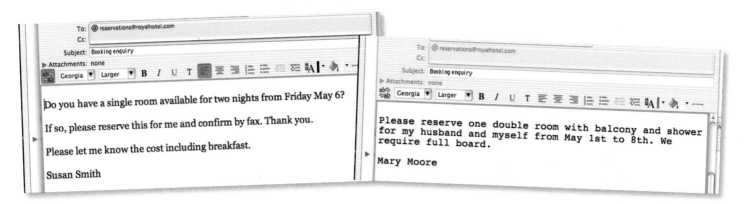

To: @ reservations@royalhotel.com
Cc:
Subject: Booking enquiry
Attachments: none

Do you have a single room available for two nights from Friday May 6?

If so, please reserve this for me and confirm by fax. Thank you.

Please let me know the cost including breakfast.

Susan Smith

To: @ reservations@royalhotel.com
Cc:
Subject: Booking enquiry
Attachments: none

Please reserve one double room with balcony and shower for my husband and myself from May 1st to 8th. We require full board.

Mary Moore

room description	101 twin beds bath, balcony	102 single bed shower	103 double bed shower	104 twin beds bath	105 double bed shower, balcony
room price	$92	$65	$85	$88	$90
Sun May 1					Mr & Mrs Moore (full board)
Mon May 2					
Tue May 3					
Wed May 4					
Thu May 5					
Fri May 6		Ms Smith (bed & breakfast)			Mr & Mrs Moore
Sat May 7					
Sun May 8		Ms Smith			

All prices include continental breakfast. For half board add $20 per person. For full board add $40 per person.

2 Look at this reply to Susan Smith's email. Find the *four* mistakes in it and correct them.

To: @ suesmith77@goodbye.com
Cc:
Subject: RE: Booking enquiry
Attachments: none

Dear Mr Smith,

Thank you for your email. I am happy to inform you that we do have a single room with shower available for you from Friday May 6 to Sunday May 8. The cost of the room with full breakfast is £65.

I can confirm that the room has been reserved for you.

We look forward to welcoming you both on May 6. Please let us know if you will be arriving later than 8 pm

Your sincerely,
A. Muster
Royal Hotel

3 Writing

Write a reply to Mrs Moore's email.

B1 You'll hear a guest booking accommodation on the phone. Listen and note down his requirements on the room chart.

2 Pronunciation

Listen to the phrases in the speech balloon and practise saying them clearly and politely.

I'll just check if we have a room available.
Yes, we do have a room free.
I'm afraid the only room we have is . . .
Could you just spell your name for me, please?
Is there a phone number where we can contact you?
What time will you be arriving, Mr Green?
We'll confirm this reservation in writing, Mrs Moore.
We'll look forward to seeing you on Monday, Ms Smith.
Thank you for your call, Mrs Moore.

3 Grammar *If . . .*

Fill the blanks in these sentences with information from your updated room chart:

1 If we move Mr and Mrs Green to room 101, they ....*won't have a double bed.*....
2 If the Greens choose full board, they ....
3 If Mr and Mrs Moore have room 101, they ....
4 If the Moores .... a room with a bath, they ....
5 If we .... Ms Smith to room 103, she ....
6 If Ms Smith .... full board, she ....

C1 Role play

👥 One of you should look at Activity 7 on page 110, the other at Activity 22 on page 118.

You'll be playing the roles of RESERVATIONS MANAGER and GUEST telephoning to reserve rooms. Update the room chart opposite. This role play is in four parts.

2 👥 Look at your updated room chart and discuss the following possible changes:

... the Browns in 104?   ... Mr Chavez in 103?   ... the Andersons in 101?
... the Andersons in 103?   ... Ms Smith in 103?   ... the Greens in 101?

Begin like this: *If we put the Browns in 104, they won't have a balcony.*

26 Checking in

A1 You'll hear two conversations recorded at the reception desk of the Seaview Hotel. Listen and fill in the missing information for each guest.

name	Mr Robert Watson
room number	....
type of room	....
cost	....
payment method	....

name	Ms Emma O'Neill
room number	....
type of room	....
cost	....
payment method	....

2 Listen again. Each receptionist made a small mistake. What were the two mistakes?

B1 Look at these phrases. Most of them are suitable for welcoming someone, but two are *not* suitable. Cross out the two that you think are unsuitable.

> Good evening, how may I help you?
> Hello, what do you want?
> It's good to see you again, Ms Black!
> It's nice to see you again, Mrs White.
> Back again, Mr Grey?
> Hello again, Ms Green, and welcome!
> Good afternoon, sir, do you have a reservation with us today?
> Good evening, Mr Brown. How nice to see you again!

2 Pronunciation

Listen to the suitable phrases and practise saying them in a polite, friendly voice.

C Role play

One of you should look at Activity 4 on page 109, the other at Activity 30 on page 122.

You'll be playing the roles of RECEPTIONIST and GUEST who has just arrived at the Royal Hotel on May 1st. This role play is in two parts.

D

This is the Royal Hotel's registration card. Fill it out with your own personal information, as if you were a guest there.

Royal Hotel

REGISTRATION CARD

Surname

Forenames

Accompanied by

Payment method: *cash* ☐   *cheque* ☐   *company account* ☐   *credit card* ☐ (No.:   )

Home address

Nationality

Passport number

Car registration number

Purpose of visit

Signature

Special requirements

Room number   Date of arrival   Date of departure

A1 You'll hear three conversations. Listen and match the names of the guests to what they require and what they want to do.

2 Listen again. How well did each of the receptionists deal with the guests?

Guest's name	What they require	What they want to do
Mr Watson	TV remote control	go for a drive
Ms O'Neill	blankets	go for a swim
Mr and Mrs Harris	towels	go shopping

B1 Vocabulary

Match the words in the list to the equipment and furniture in the pictures.

balcony   bathtub   bedspread   bidet   desk   dressing table   faucets (taps)
hair-dryer   light switch   mini-bar   mirror   night stand (bedside table)   pillow
radiator   radio-alarm   reading light   sheets   shower   sofa   towels   waste bin

Which equipment and furniture is *not* shown in the pictures?

2 Grammar *Prepositions*

Write your answers to these questions about the photos.

1 Where's the balcony?   *It's outside the room through the glass door.*

2 Where's the vase of flowers? ....

3 Where's the picture? ....

4 Where are the towels? ....

5 Where's the sofa? ....

6 Where are the mirrors? ....

C You'll hear two people talking about the facilities that their hotel offers.

Listen and tick (✓) the boxes to show which facilities each hotel offers.

		CENTRAL HOTEL	BELLEVUE HOTEL
ROOMS			
🛁	bath	☐	☐
🚿	shower	☐	☐
	hair-dryer	☐	☐
☎	telephone	☐	☐
	desk	☐	☐
📺	TV	☐	☐
HOTEL FACILITIES			
	indoor pool	☐	☐
	outdoor pool	☐	☐
	fitness centre	☐	☐
	sauna	☐	☐
🅿	car park	☐	☐
🅿	garage	☐	☐
	tennis court	☐	☐
	garden	☐	☐
	play area	☐	☐
	beach	☐	☐
	water sports	☐	☐
✕	restaurant	☐	☐
	night club	☐	☐
🍸	cocktail bar	☐	☐
	bar and lounge	☐	☐
	conference facilities	☐	☐

D Role play

👥 Take it in turns to play the roles of a MEMBER OF THE HOTEL STAFF and a GUEST.

Imagine that the guest is being shown the room and its facilities in the photos opposite. Explain where everything in the room is, and how it works.

Here we are, this is your room: number 101.
The door locks like this . . .
And over here is the . . .
It works like this . . .
If you want to adjust the . . .

...and here is the balcony.

A1 You'll hear some guests asking for information. Listen and tick (✓) the boxes to show the right answers.

1 The first guest wants to know ...
when lunch starts. ☐   when lunch ends. ☐
The receptionist advises him to ...
reserve a table. ☐   get there early. ☐

2 The second guest wants to know where she can buy ...
a gift. ☐   sun lotion. ☐
The pool attendant ...
gives her a towel. ☐   doesn't give her a towel. ☐

3 The third guest wants to ...
order today's special. ☐   find out about today's special. ☐
The waitress recommends ...
the special. ☐   another dish. ☐

4 The fourth guest wants to get a ticket for ...
a concert. ☐   the opera. ☐
The hall porter (concierge) tells her that she should ...
pay him for the ticket now. ☐   not pay him for the ticket. ☐

5 The fifth guest wants to know ...
where he can wash clothes. ☐   how to get his washing done. ☐
The housekeeper tells him to put his dry-cleaning in ...
the same bag. ☐   a different bag. ☐

2 Listen again. Pay attention to the tone of voice the members of staff use and tick the boxes to show how they sound.

The receptionist sounds ...	helpful	☐	unhelpful	☐
The pool attendant sounds ...	helpful	☐	unhelpful	☐
The waitress sounds ...	efficient	☐	inefficient	☐
The hall porter sounds ...	friendly	☐	unfriendly	☐
The housekeeper sounds ...	friendly	☐	unfriendly	☐

B1 Look at the phrases in the speech balloon. Match them to the situations in which you would say them.

Situations

1 If you know the answer to a question …
2 If you have to check before answering a question …
3 If you can't answer a question …
4 If you want to give someone some extra information …

> *Certainly, I'll just explain …*
> *Excuse me a moment, I'll have to check.*
> *I'll just have to find out.*
> *I'm afraid I don't know.*
> *I'm not quite sure, I'm afraid.*
> *I'm sorry, I don't really know.*
> *Just one moment, please, I'll ask one of my colleagues.*
> *Yes, certainly. Well, …*
> *By the way, you might be interested to know that …*

2 Pronunciation

Listen to the phrases and practise saying them in a friendly and helpful voice.

C Role play

Half of the members of the class should look at Activity 11 on page 113, the others at Activity 26 on page 121.

You will be playing the roles of GUEST and RECEPTIONIST at the Hotel Miramar. This role play is in four parts.

> *Can you help me, please? I'd like to know …*
> *I wonder if it's possible for me to …*
> *Can you tell me …?*

> *Yes, certainly, there's a flight …*
> *I'm afraid it's not possible to …*
> *Yes, certainly, one moment please …*

29 The best hotel for you ...

A1 Read the accommodation descriptions of hotels in St Lucia. Which place ...

doesn't charge for excursions? ....
has its own dive school? ....
has most organised activities? ....
serves free champagne? ....

has free water-skiing? ....
has the fewest rooms? ....
has the most rooms? ....
has the best food? ....

2 Choose one place where you'd most like to spend two weeks' vacation.
Highlight the features of the place that you find attractive.

3 Discuss these questions:

● Which of the places would you prefer to stay at? Why?
● What do you think is the worst thing about each place?
● What do you think is the best thing about each one?
● If you wanted to experience the atmosphere of a country and meet the people, which place would be best?

B1 Which would be the best place for these people
to stay? Why?

Mr and Mrs Brown (both aged 65) They haven't travelled abroad before.

Mr and Mrs Black (both aged 30) This is their honeymoon.

The Greens (father, 35, mother, 33, daughter, 12, son, 8) They want to be active on their holiday.

Ms Grey (aged 25) She is travelling alone but wants to make friends on holiday.

2 Role play

Take it in turns to play the roles
of a TRAVEL AGENT* and one of the
CLIENTS in the pictures. Discuss which
hotel is the best for the client.

* If you're the travel agent, you can find
more information about each hotel in
Activity 36 on page 125.

> If you stay at . . . you'll be able to . . .
> The best things about . . . are . . .
> I think you'll find that . . . is better
>   for you because . . .
> Another nice thing about that
>   hotel is . . .

> I really want somewhere with
>   a swimming pool.
> . . . looks very nice.
> Which do you recommend?

ALL INCLUSIVE
Club St. Lucia By Splash
FOR FAMILIES, COUPLES, AND SINGLES OF ANY AGE

Location Club St. Lucia by Splash lies on 65 acres of the Cap Estate on a picturesque bay about 1½ hours drive from the International Airport.

Facilities Club St. Lucia by Splash is made up of five colourful villages, one of which accommodates adults over 18. There are impressive swimming pools, one with separate children's section and waterslide, the St. Lucia Racquet Club with championship tennis courts and fitness room, a spa and a wide variety of watersports. Golf is available at the Cap Estate Golf Club close by. There are extensive children's facilities including an airconditioned nursery, children's clubs, playgrounds and a fun children's restaurant. For dining there's a choice of restaurants including a pizza/pasta restaurant, an oriental restaurant and a romantic oceanside setting serving dinner to adults only. There's a number of bars, and regular evening entertainment is provided.

Accommodation 369 rooms located in cottages set around the gardens, each with airconditioning, coffee maker, telephone, television, bath, shower and terrace. Standard rooms (STD): as above.

ALL INCLUSIVE
East Winds Inn
FOR FAMILIES, COUPLES, AND SINGLES OF ANY AGE

Location East Winds is on a small, secluded, golden sandy beach with its charming cottages scattered in lush tropical gardens. East Winds is about 1½ hours from the airport.

Facilities A tropical hideaway offering obliging personal service and outstanding cuisine under the guidance of the hotel's award winning chef. There is a pool with swim-up bar, as well as a further bar and restaurant on the beach. Limited watersports are available from here. The evenings are quiet with regular entertainment while guests enjoy superb meals in a relaxed and romantic atmosphere, before and afterwards in the elegant club house and its bar.

Family saver rooms (SAV): as standard but can accommodate two adults plus two children under 6 years of age.
Romance rooms (ROM): for adults only with four poster or two queen beds, and hammock on terrace.
Family suites (FMS): as standard with airconditioned bedroom, living area with ceiling fan and a terrace.
Deluxe oceanview (DOV): four poster bed, jacuzzi bath, and just a few yards from the beach with seaview.

Your holiday includes:
- All meals and snacks daily, local drinks by the glass.
- Watersports, including sunfish sailing, paddle boats, snorkelling, windsurfing, kayaking, waterskiing plus group instruction, introductory pool scuba lesson.
- Tennis (day and night) including two group tennis clinics per stay, aerobics studio and fitness centre.
- Bicycles on property, jogging trail.
- For children 3 months to 3 years there's a nursery, for 4–12 year olds there are daily children's clubs and for teenagers, there's beach volleyball, tennis, as well as watersports.
- Backgammon, shuffle-board, table tennis, volleyball.
- Nightly entertainment, theme nights, disco.
- All porterage, taxes, service charges, tips (excludes overseas airport departure tax).

Accommodation 30 spacious rooms in semi detached cottages set in the gardens, cooled by ceiling fan and sea breezes. All have tea and coffee making facilities, shower, telephone, fridge (stocked daily with soft drinks and beer), twin or one kingsize bed.
Superior cottages (SUP): rondavel rooms, facilities as above with semi circular shaded terrace.
Deluxe cottages (DLX): as above, with larger bathroom, television, inhouse movies and large terrace.
Oceanview rooms (OV): facilities as above, smaller but with balcony and great seaview.
Mini suite: available on request.

Your holiday includes:
- All meals: full breakfast, lunch and dinner, including picnic hampers and afternoon tea.
- All drinks by the glass, including champagne served every evening.
- Manager's cocktail party once a week.
- Dine-around meal plan once a week at local restaurants (drinks and transport at extra cost).
- Watersports: pedalos, snorkelling, aquaboards and canoes.
- Board games and videos (in deluxe and oceanfront rooms only).
- Regular evening entertainment with soft live music.
- All porterage, taxes and service charges (excludes overseas airport departure tax).

Anse Chastanet

Location Nestling within a 600 acre plantation on St. Lucia's southwest coast, this gem Anse Chastanet is 15 minutes drive from Soufrière and about 1 hour from the airport. A lot of steps from the beach to some rooms makes Anse Chastanet unsuitable for those with walking difficulties.

Facilities Dining here is in the hilltop restaurant with incredible views of St. Lucia's beautiful sunsets, or down at the beachside restaurant where dress is always casual. Life at Anse Chastanet centres around the beach, where guests can enjoy free snorkelling, windsurfing, kyaks and mini sailing. Anse Chastanet is located in the heart of St Lucia's marine reserves and for divers there's a PADI dive school right on the beach, (certified divers can pre-book a 12 dive package for £175) and beginners can join a free resort course before venturing out to explore. On land the hotel organises select free excursions, as well as rain forest hikes, nature walks and superb biking on its unique 12 miles of private trails through tropical jungle (biking at extra cost). Complimentary water taxis are available to take guests to Soufrière and the hotel's second secluded beach. The resort also has two small shops, a library, art gallery and a full service spa offering body and beauty treatments at extra cost.

Accommodation Rooms (49) are beautiful, unique and traditionally decorated, each has ceiling fan, fridge, tea/coffee making facilities, shower, and an incredible view! Kuoni clients will receive a complimentary stocked mini bar (soft drinks) and fruit basket on arrival.
Superior hillside rooms (SUP): in octagonal cottages on the hill with wrap around balconies with Piton or ocean views.
Deluxe beachside rooms (BCH): are very private, with garden view and immediate access onto the beach.
Deluxe hillside rooms (DLX): are very spacious with a huge bathroom, large balconies and some with open walls. The views of the ocean and/or Pitons are absolutely breathtaking!

A1 Look at the information opposite and find the answers to these questions:

1 How can you get to Pangkor Laut Resort?

2 Are there any permanent residents on the island?

3 Altogether, how many suites and villas are there in the resort?

4 How many different places serve food or beverages?

2 Discuss these questions:

● What do you think are the most attractive features of Pangkor Laut Resort?

● If you were a guest at Pangkor Laut Resort, which of the facilities would you use?

B Imagine that you are designing your own new two- or three-star hotel, with all the facilities you think it should have. Before you start, fill in the blanks in 1 and 2 with some more ideas of your own.

1 First of all, decide on the following:

The **location** of your hotel:

    beach   city centre   city outskirts   lakeside   ....

The **guests** you're expecting:

    businesspeople   budget travellers   families on vacation   ....

2 Now decide what facilities you want to offer. This isn't Pangkor Laut Resort, so you can't offer the same wide range of luxury facilities — your budget limits you to five!

Room facilities: (five only)

    satellite TV with English-language channels   fax phone   balcony or terrrace
    sunbeds on the balcony or terrace   desk and chairs   armchairs   mini-bar
    24-hour room service   air conditioning   ....

Public facilities: (five only)

    indoor pool   fitness centre   outdoor heated pool   TV room   tennis court   golf course
    sauna   sailing   water-skiing   children's playroom   coffee shop   bar   lounge
    sunbathing area   garden   ....

3 Draw a plan of the hotel, showing where the public facilities will be located. Then draw a plan of a guest room, showing how it will be designed.

4 Prepare a presentation of your ideas, which you will give to the rest of the class.

5 *Whole-class activity* Each team presents its design to the rest of the class. Vote on the most imaginative design.

C Writing

Write a description of your hotel, using the Pangkor Laut Resort information as your model.

LOCATION

4° 14" North by 100° 34" East is our address.

Pangkor Laut is a privately-owned island off the west coast of Peninsular Malaysia facing the Straits of Malacca. There are only two ways to get here; one by private ferry from the peaceful town of Lumut on the mainland; the other by plane to Pangkor Island and a shorter boat journey across the historic Straits.

ONE ISLAND

Virtually the whole of the 300-acre island is covered in virgin rainforest estimated to be more than two million years old with magnificent sweeping bays of fine sandy beaches along its perimeters. Our island is large enough to sustain an abundance of wildlife yet small enough to have escaped man's exploitation.

The island's population is limited to guests and staff; for on this one island is only one resort. The island is traversed by jungle trails culminating at many of the bays along the island's perimeter. Nature lovers will encounter a variety of species of colourful birds and plants including native orchids. Yellow pied hornbills, white-breasted sea eagles, crab-eating macaque monkeys and tropical iguanas are common sights.

ONE RESORT

At Pangkor Laut Resort, you can live over the water, on the beach or up on the hillside amidst the jungle. Each promises discreet luxury with panoramic views of the sea and the virgin jungle. 125 luxury villas on Royal Bay comprising ninety-four Royal Hill Villas perched dramatically on the hillside amidst the rainforest with sweeping views of the sea below; eight Royal Beach Villas clustered around tropical gardens steps away from the fine sandy beach as well as twenty-one Sea Villas and two Royal Sea Villa Suites set on stilts over the emerald green sea and linked by wooden walkways.

This is a nature resort and hideaway for those who want to experience a pristine wilderness of peace and tranquillity. Pangkor Laut Resort promises to be a world away from it all. Unrivalled luxury amidst unmatched natural beauty.

DINING AND ENTERTAINMENT

The Palm Grove Café offers casual all-day dining comprising local as well as Continental dishes. The Samudra Restaurant serves a unique blending of Malaysian and Mediterranean cuisines in a spectacular over-water setting. The Royal Bay Beach Club overlooking our 35-metre lap pool and tennis courts offers poolside snacks and platters to accompany a round of drinks in a dramatic setting. The Oasis Bar on the deck of our freeform pool offers drinks and Tropical Cocktails. Chapmans Bar located beachfront at Emerald Bay offers light lunches or snacks, allowing you to spend the day at our little piece of heaven.

RECREATIONAL FACILITIES

Recreation facilities include 3 tennis and 2 squash courts; 2 swimming pools; hot spa and cold dip; a fully-equipped water sports centre including snorkelling, windsurfing, sailing, water-skiing, scuba diving with recognised certificate; fishing trips; fitness centre/gymnasium; sauna; a television lounge for news, films and documentaries; a multilingual library; a gift and sundries shop; a conference/meeting room; jungle trekking as well as cruises for charter to neighbouring islands on one of the Resort's many vessels.

A1

You'll hear some interviews with people who receive payment. What are the most common forms of payment that their guests and clients use? Listen and fill the blanks in these sentences:

> ▶ by credit card: VISA MasterCard
>
> ▶ by charge card: AMERICAN EXPRESS DINERS Club International
>
> ▶ by debit card: Maestro DELTA
>
> ▶ with traveller's cheques
> ▶ with a personal cheque (or Eurocheque)
> ▶ with a voucher (from a tour operator or travel agent)
> ▶ in cash
> ▶ in another currency

1 Jane works for an airline. Most passengers pay .... but she also accepts foreign .... — but not ....

2 Rod is a travel agent. .... to .... % of his customers pay .... over the .... or in the shop.

3 Janine is a travel agent. Her customers usually pay .... This enables them to spread the .... of their holiday using .... facilities.

4 Tom works in a sports store. Most of his customers pay .... for purchases under $............. . They also use .... and receive their .... in cash. He won't accept foreign ....

5 Fiona is a waitress. Her younger customers pay .... and the older ones ....

2

How do clients usually pay in hotels, restaurants, travel agents and shops in *your* country?

B1

What is the average price of each of these goods and services in your country?

2 Role play

👥 If a tourist asks you the price of the goods and services above, what do you say to him or her? Role play the conversation between a TOURIST and a LOCAL RESIDENT. Then change roles.

> What does a . . . cost?
> A . . . costs about . . .
> The average price of . . . is . . .
> That costs between . . . and . . .
> You can pay up to . . . for that.
> It depends whether you
>   buy it in a . . . or in a . . .

C1 You'll hear some prices being quoted. Write down each price.

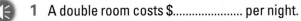

1 A double room costs $..................... per night.

2 A round trip to Melbourne costs $..................... .

3 The set meal costs $..................... .

4 An all day ticket costs $..................... .

5 The taxi will cost about $..................... .

6 Airport tax is $..................... extra.

7 A one-way ticket costs ¥..................... .

8 You have been overcharged by $..................... .

2 Pronunciation

Listen to these prices and practise saying them:

1 $15.99

2 NZ $115

3 A$150

4 SFr 125

5 $17.70

6 ¥31,200

7 $116

8 160 Saudi riyals

D Role play

One of you should look at Activity 14 on page 114, the other at Activity 32 on page 123.

You'll be playing the roles of CASHIER and CLIENT.
This role play is in two parts.

So that's . . . altogether.
That'll be . . . altogether.
So the total is . . .
Oh, no, sorry. That should be . . .

I'm sorry, how much did you say that was?
Sorry, could you say that again, please?
I'm not sure that's quite right.

A1 👥 **Which countries use these currencies? Match the currencies to the countries:**

baht   dollars   forints   francs   pesos   rands   ringgits   roubles   rupees   yen
Canada   Hungary   India   Japan   Malaysia   Mexico   Russia   South Africa   Switzerland   Thailand

2 **What currency do the following countries use?**

Austria   Belgium   Finland   France   Germany   Greece   Ireland   Italy   Luxembourg   Portugal
Spain   The Netherlands

3 Some of the currencies listed are used in other countries, too. Do you know where they are used?

> They use dollars in New Zealand, I think.
> — And in Singapore, too.

4 Which are the Top 5 nationalities who visit your country (or your place of work)?

● What currencies do they each use?
● What were the exchange rates yesterday?

Fill out the chart.

Nationality	Currency	Exchange rate
1		
2		
3		
4		
5		

B **1** You'll hear some tourists changing money. Listen and note down how much each one gets.

The first client changes SFr............................ and gets $............................ .

The second client changes ¥............................ and gets $............................ .

The third client changes Singapore $............................ and NZ $............................
and gets US $............................ .

The fourth client buys $............................ and pays ¥............................ .

2 If the same clients wanted to change the same money today, what would they get? Look at the exchange rates in a recent newspaper to find out.

3 Role play

👥 Role play a series of transactions where a TOURIST wants a CASHIER to change these sums of money into *your* currency. Use the real exchange rates from a recent newspaper. (You may need a calculator for this role play.)

Traveller's cheques:

200 US dollars	350 Australian dollars	1,000 South African rand
200 Canadian dollars	310 Swiss francs	

Cash:

50 Canadian dollars	100,000 Japanese yen
50 New Zealand dollars	100 Swiss francs

C **1** 👥 Here are some situations you might find yourself in. What would you do? What would you say to each client?

HOTEL GUEST:	*My Visa card expires tomorrow.*
RESTAURANT GUEST:	*I seem to have forgotten my wallet.*
CLIENT IN TRAVEL AGENCY:	*Is it all right if I pay you tomorrow?*
HOTEL GUEST:	*I was expecting a 25 per cent discount on my bill, but you haven't given me any discount.*
CUSTOMER IN SHOP: 1	*I'm afraid I only have dollars, not local currency.*
CUSTOMER IN SHOP: 2	*$99? Is that your best price?*
CUSTOMER IN SHOP: 3	*I can get the same thing round the corner for $10 less.*
CUSTOMER IN SHOP: 4	*Do you take Japanese yen traveller's cheques?*

> *I'm very sorry, sir, but . . .*
> *I'm sorry about that, madam. I'm afraid . . .*
> *Yes, that's no problem at all, sir.*
> *Well, I'm afraid that makes it rather difficult. You see . . .*

2 Role play

Join a different partner Role play the problem situations you discussed in C1. Take it in turns to be the CLIENT.

33 Explaining the bill

A You'll hear a guest checking out of a hotel. The cashier explains the extra charges on the bill. Listen and note down the reasons for the charges on the guest's bill.

Sunset
BEACH RESORT

DATE	REFERENCE	DESCRIPTION	AMOUNT
05 Jan	4668	PALM BEACH *Drinks at the bar*	7.50
05 Jan	1955	SPORTS *Tennis court hire*	12.00
05 Jan	R 101	BERMUDA PLAN	180.00
06 Jan	3891	POOL SIDE	6.30
06 Jan	12345	TELEX & FAX	18.00
06 Jan	3291	ROOM SERVICE	10.00
06 Jan	4668	PALM BEACH	5.50
06 Jan	9832	COFFEE HSE	12.00
06 Jan	1291	WTR SPORTS	15.00
06 Jan	R 101	BERMUDA PLAN	180.00
07 Jan	3892	POOL SIDE	8.00
07 Jan	29871	PALM BEACH	9.00
07 Jan	12010	MISCELLANEOUS	15.00
07 Jan	R 101	BERMUDA PLAN	180.00
		BALANCE DUE....	658.30
		SUMMARY OF CHARGES:	
	3	PALM BEACH POSTING(S) =	22.00
	1	SPORTS POSTING(S) =	12.00
	2	POOL SIDE POSTING(S) =	14.30
	1	TELEX & FAX POSTING(S) =	18.00
	1	ROOM SERVICE POSTING(S) =	10.00
	1	WTR SPORTS POSTING(S) =	15.00
	3	ROOM CHARGE POSTING(S) =	540.00
	1	COFFEE HSE POSTING(S) =	12.00
	1	MISCELLANEOUS POSTING(S) =	15.00

B Role play

Imagine that a cashier is explaining this bill to a guest. Take it in turns to play the roles of the CASHIER and the GUEST, changing roles when you reach the second part of the bill.

> What's this charge for?

> Well, let me explain . . .
> This charge is for . . .
> The next item on the bill is . . .
> And this is the service charge at . . .
>   per cent, making a total of . . .

Central Hotel

DATE	REFERENCE	DESCRIPTION	AMOUNT
11 Jul	124	RESTAURANT	48.90
11 Jul	R 312	ROOM CHARGE (CONTINENTAL PLAN)	120.00
11 Jul	R 312	TELEPHONE	2.40
11 Jul	028	CAR HIRE	94.50
11 Jul	983	TV/VIDEO	10.00
11 Jul	182	COCKTAIL BAR	9.50
11 Jul	R 312	MINIBAR	5.00
11 Jul	127	RESTAURANT	67.00

12 Jul	R 312	ROOM CHARGE (CONTINENTAL PLAN)	120.00
12 Jul	381	COFFEE SHOP	8.50
12 Jul	781	OPERA TICKETS	78.00
12 Jul	104	NEWSPAPERS & MAGAZINES	2.80
12 Jul	351	TOILETRIES	4.20
13 Jul	129	TENNIS	12.50
13 Jul	R 312	MINIBAR	5.20
13 Jul	R 312	ROOM CHARGE (CONTINENTAL PLAN)	120.00
13 Jul	983	TV/VIDEO	10.00
13 Jul	356	GIFT SHOP	45.99

SUB TOTAL....		764.49
SERVICE CHARGE ℗ 12.5%	95.56	
LOCAL TAXES ℗ 2.5%	19.11	
BALANCE DUE....		879.16

C Role play

One of you should look at Activity 10 on page 112, the other at Activity 25 on page 120.

You'll be role playing a restaurant situation. The WAITER/WAITRESS presents the bill to a GUEST, explains the items on it and then receives payment.
This role play is in two parts.

> Here's your bill (check), sir.
> It comes to . . . altogether.
> Well, if you remember, you had two . . . at $2.50 each.
> The total includes/doesn't include service.
> And here's your change.
>   Thank you very much, madam.

34. Is service included?

A1 You'll hear three people talking about tipping in the USA, the UK and France. Listen and fill in the missing information on the chart.

Will they expect a tip? How much should I give?					
	USA	UK	France	Japan	Australia
Waiter/Waitress		10–15%			
Barman/Barmaid					
Hotel porter				nothing	
Hotel maid					
Taxi driver					

2 How much should the client give each person for service in *your* country?

3 Read these texts about Japan and Australia and fill in the missing information in the chart above.

JAPAN has the distinction of being one of the few developed countries where tipping is not generally expected, even at places like restaurants, hotels, etc. If a service charge is expected, it will automatically be added to your bill (another way of saying it is compulsory); this may be found at hotels and restaurants. Quite separate from the service charge, by the way, is the 10 per cent tax incurred if a restaurant or bar bill exceeds ¥5,000 or a hotel bill exceeds ¥10,000. This can sometimes be avoided by asking for separate bills if there are two or more of you.

TIPPING is not usually expected in Australia, except in restaurants where you should add 10% to the bill for good service. Even a taxi driver doesn't expect a tip, but it is customary to round the fare up to the nearest dollar.

B1   Do this survey with your partners.

In your country, which of these people would you tip? How much would you give them?

Fill in the chart with the names of the people in your group. Use this system:

✓   = 'I usually give a tip.'
✗   = 'I never give a tip.'
?   = 'I sometimes give a tip.'
10%   = I give ten per cent of the bill.' (or whatever exact percentage you give)
± 15% = 'I give about fifteen per cent of the bill.' (or whatever)
50¢   = 'I give fifty cents.' (or whatever)
↗   = 'I round the bill up to a slightly higher sum.' (e.g. from $19.50 to $20)

Your partners' names:				
barman/barmaid				
bus conductor				
fast food server				
cinema attendant				
flight attendant				
hairdresser				
hotel porter				
pool attendant				
room maid				
toilet attendant				
waiter/waitress				

2   Compare your answers. Who are the 'Top 3 tip receivers'?

3 Role play

Imagine that you're giving advice to a Japanese or Australian VISITOR to your country. Where are clients expected to give a tip, and how much is expected? Where are service charges *included* in the bill? Role play the conversation and then change roles.

4 Writing

Write a paragraph for foreign visitors explaining when and how much to tip in your country.

"Damn – I forgot to tip the waiter."

A1 Read the information about Tokyo Narita Airport. What would you say to a client who asks these questions:

1 How long does it take to get from the airport to downtown Tokyo by train?
2 How much does the taxi ride cost?
3 Is it a good idea to take the bus to the centre?
4 How much time should I allow to make my connection with an internal flight?
5 What's the best way to get to downtown Tokyo from the airport?

TOKYO NARITA

Narita International Airport is 65 km east of downtown Tokyo. The taxi ride takes at least 90 minutes, but much longer at busy times of day (and it costs a small fortune). Far cheaper than a taxi is the Airport Limousine Bus, which will take you to the Tokyo City Air Terminal. The JR Narita Express (N'EX) train goes to Tokyo Station in downtown Tokyo and takes about an hour (reservation essential). The Keisei Skyliner train to Keisei Ueno Station also takes about an hour. Both Tokyo and Ueno stations are on the Yamanote loop line which runs all round central Tokyo, but this is not recommended if you have heavy baggage.

Most Japanese domestic flights leave from Haneda Airport (80 km away on the other side of the city). The inter-airport bus takes at least 2 hours at busy times, so it may be quicker to take the JR Narita Express to Shinagawa Station (beyond Tokyo Station) and then transfer to the Keikyu Line for another train to Haneda in about two hours. The Keikyu Airport Express also links the two airports in about two hours, but the service is not very frequent.

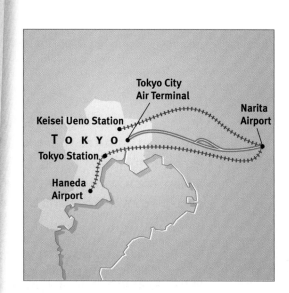

2 You'll hear three conversations at a travel agent's. The clients are finding out how to get to and from John F. Kennedy Airport in New York. Listen and match the answers to the questions.

Questions	Answers
1 How long does it take by subway to Manhattan?	15 minutes
2 How long does it take by Carey Airport Express bus?	20 minutes
3 The Carey Airport Express buses run every …	30 minutes
4 How long does it take by Gray Line Air Shuttle?	1 hour
5 How long does it take by taxi to Manhattan — if you're lucky?	$1\frac{1}{4}$ hours
6 How long does it take by taxi to Manhattan — if you're unlucky?	$1\frac{1}{2}$ hours
7 How long does it take by helicopter?	2 hours

B1 Think about your own town or city and discuss these questions:

- Where is the nearest international airport?
- Where is the nearest main train station?
- How do you get to the airport from your school, college or place of work by bus or train?
- How do you get to the main train station?
- What routes would you take to the airport and station by car?

2 Role play

Take it in turns to play the roles of a VISITOR and a LOCAL RESIDENT.

VISITOR Play two of the roles shown in the pictures Ask the local resident these questions:

> How do I get to the airport from here?
> What's the best way to get to the train station from here?

> The best thing to do …
> The quickest way to get to …
> If you take the … it'll take about … minutes and it'll cost …
> It's not a good idea to … because … [give reason]

LOCAL RESIDENT Answer the visitor's questions.

36 Local knowledge

A1 You'll hear two information officers talking about the questions that people ask them. Write down the questions they're asked.

1 The most common question that the man is asked is:

.... ?

2 The most common question that the woman is asked is:

.... ?

3 The most difficult question that the man has been asked was:

.... ?

4 The most difficult question that the woman has been asked was:

.... ?

5 The most unusual question that the man has been asked was:

.... ?

6 The most unusual question that the woman has been asked was:

.... ?

2 What other common questions do you think people ask in a Tourist Information Centre?

B You'll hear another information officer talking to three different visitors. Listen and fill in the missing information.

Bus or metro tickets
Price: ....
Where to buy them: ....

Bank opening hours
Monday to Friday: ....
Saturday: ....
Sunday: ....
Other places to change money: ....

Department stores opening hours
Monday to Friday: ....
Saturday: ....
Sunday: ....

👥 Compare your answers.

C1 👤👤👤👤 How much do you know about your own town or city? Make notes below. You may have to do some research.

TRANSPORTATION

Bus, tram or metro tickets
  where to buy them:....................................... cost: ....
  how to have tickets validated:..
  how to transfer from one route to another:..
Taxis
  phone numbers:................... fares:............. how much to tip: ....
Trains (or buses) to two other cities
  times:...
  cost:...
  how to reserve seats:...

OPENING TIMES   Monday to Friday   Saturday
  Shops and stores   from .... to ....   from .... to ....
  Supermarkets   from .... to ....   from .... to ....
  Banks   from .... to ....   from .... to ....
                                                               from .... to ....

TOURIST ATTRACTIONS
  top three tourist attractions in the area: ticket prices:

  ....

  ....

  ....

  Three more useful pieces of information about your city
  or region which a foreign visitor needs to know:

  ....

  ....

  ....

---

2   Role play

👤👤 Take it in turns to play the roles of a TOURIST and an INFORMATION OFFICER at your local tourist information office. Role play a series of conversations. The tourist asks for some of the information you noted down in C1.

> ...doesn't open until ...
> A ticket costs about ...
> The last ... leaves at ...
> They're open from ... to ...
> It's cheaper to go by ...
> If you miss the last ... you'll have to ...

A1

You'll hear four guests talking to a receptionist at a hotel. Listen and tick the boxes to show what the receptionist offers to do for each of them.

1 The receptionist offers to …
phone the railway station for Mr White. ☐
reserve a seat on the train for Mr White. ☐

2 She offers to …
lend Mrs Brown a swimsuit. ☐   sell Mrs Brown a swimsuit. ☐

3 She offers to …
send a fax for Miss Green. ☐
show Miss Green how to operate the fax machine. ☐

4 She offers to …
provide a new clock-radio for Mr Black. ☐   give Mr Black a wake-up call. ☐

2 👥 **Listen again and discuss these questions:**

● Which guest was the receptionist least polite to?
● Which of her ideas was the least sensible, do you think?

3 👥 **Decide together what you would offer to do for a guest who . . .**

wants to know what's on at the theatre or opera this weekend.

tells you that the bulb in his reading light is broken.

tells you that her room overlooking the street is noisy.

is leaving the hotel at 4am.

needs a taxi to the airport at 4am.

only has a large denomination banknote in your currency and wants to change it.

4 Role play

Join a different partner Take it in turns to play the roles of a GUEST and a MEMBER OF STAFF.

GUEST   Explain to the member of staff what your problem is (from the list in **A3**). After he or she has offered to help you, say 'Thank you'.

MEMBER OF STAFF   Offer to help the guest, using some of the expressions in the speech balloon.

> If you can't do something a client asks you to do, it's important to sound polite when you refuse. And explain why you can't do what they ask.

> Good morning. How may I help you?
> I'll ask . . . to . . . for you.
> Would you like me to . . . for you?
> I could . . . for you, if you like.
> Shall I . . . for you?
> I could either . . . or . . . Which would you prefer me to do?
> I'm afraid there's nothing I can do. Sorry.

Whenever you're asking clients and guests to do something, you need to sound polite, of course. But if you want them to do something they don't want to do, you need to be extra polite — and you should also explain why you'd like them to do what you ask.

B1 Grammar *to.../...-ing*

Using the phrases in the speech balloon, write down what you'd say if you wanted a client to, or not to ...

1 move her car.
2 pay in cash.
3 show you his driving licence.
4 wait a moment.
5 sit there.

Excuse me. Would you mind ... -ing ...?
I'm sorry, but could I ask you to ..., please?
Excuse me. Would you mind not ...-ing?
I'm sorry, but could I ask you not to ..., please?

2

Tick the reason which sounds more polite for each request in B1.

1 because it's blocking the exit. ☐   because you can't park it there. ☐
2 because it's only $3. ☐   because we only accept credit cards for amounts over $10. ☐
3 because I need to make a note of the number. ☐   because I want to see if it's valid. ☐
4 because there are no tables free. ☐   because we aren't ready for you yet. ☐
5 because this table is reserved. ☐   because I want some other people to sit here. ☐

C Role play

Imagine that you are in each of these situations. What would you say to the clients? Take it turns to play the roles of a CLIENT and a MEMBER OF STAFF.

I'm sorry to have to ask you this, but ...
Would you mind moving your car, please?

38 Car rental

A You'll hear a car rental clerk dealing with a client who wants to rent a car. Listen and fill out the form with the client's requirements.

> Name . . . .
>   *title*   *first name*   *family name*
> Car required: Group . . . . Make . . . .
> Full insurance required?   Yes ☐   No ☐
> Unlimited mileage?   Yes ☐   No ☐
> From . . . .
>   *time*   *day*   *month*   *year*
> To . . . .
>   *time*   *day*   *month*   *year*
> Pick-up location . . . .
> Return location . . . .

B Fill the blanks in this dialogue. Then listen and compare your answers with the model version.

CLERK: *Good morning. How can I help you?* . . . .

CLIENT: Good morning. Can I arrange car rental here?

CLERK : . . . .

CLIENT : For three days, starting tomorrow morning.

CLERK : . . . .

CLIENT : I don't really mind, but I only need a small one.

CLERK : . . . .

CLIENT : That sounds fine. How much will it cost?

CLERK : . . . .

CLIENT : Does that include all the extras?

CLERK : . . . .

CLIENT : Excellent! Well, can we do the paperwork now, to save time tomorrow?

CLERK : . . . .

CLIENT : Good. Right, here's my driver's licence and my passport.

CLERK : . . . .

CLIENT : By Visa — here's my card . . .

C Look at the information in the text opposite, which is from a brochure for holidays in Greece. Then answer the questions below the text.

Car Hire

Leave the local bus timetables behind. Make the most of your holiday! Book a car and give yourself the freedom to find secluded beaches, unspoilt villages and rural landscapes. It's the key to real holiday independence. What's more, hiring a car can be excellent value for money, and if four of you share, it could set you back just about the same as public transport. First Choice have arranged pre-bookable car hire at special rates for rentals of either 3 or 7 days. By booking in advance, you'll know just what the deal is.

Car Hire Prices include:

- Unlimited mileage.
- Insurance for fire and theft and third party cover.
- Collision Damage Waiver (this means you are protected, subject to any excess for which you may be responsible, against the cost of any damage to the car, regardless of the cause but excluding theft, attempted theft and vandalism).
- Maintenance and replacement in case of breakdown.
- Local taxes (excluding local taxes on some extras which are payable locally).
- Delivery/collection during office hours.

Car Hire Prices Do Not include:

- Personal Accident Insurance which can be arranged and paid for in resort. (If you have taken First Choice Travel Insurance, you are covered as outlined on page 328.)
- Car contents insurance, garaging, refuelling charges, parking and traffic fines.
- Delivery/collection for out of office hours, which may incur a local charge.
- Optional extras such as baby seats (approximately 500 drachmas a day), roof racks, etc. These extras must be requested at the time of making your booking and are paid for in resort.
- Petrol deposit of approximately 1,000 drachmas for a full tank of petrol which will be taken at the time of hire and refunded if the car is returned with the same amount of fuel.
- Charges for additional drivers.

Driver Requirements

- Drivers must have a full UK licence and a minimum 1 year's experience. Minimum driving age 21.

DO REMEMBER TO TAKE YOUR DRIVING LICENCE WITH YOU.

General Information

- Cars will normally be delivered to your hotel or apartment between 9am to 12 noon on the first day of hire and should be returned or ready for collection by 8pm on the last day of hire. If you wish to collect your car on arrival at the

resort airport, please make this known at the time of booking.
- On delivery of the car, the driver(s) will be asked to sign the car hire company's terms of hire, making the rental the subject of a direct contract between the car hire company and the driver. The vehicle may only be driven by persons authorised in advance.

How to Book

It couldn't be easier! Just reserve your car at the time of making your holiday booking; your car hire arrangements and price will then be confirmed on your holiday invoice. You will receive a car hire voucher, along with your documents, about three weeks before your departure. This voucher must be handed to the car hire company as proof of reservation when you collect the car.

1 Do I have to pay for each kilometre?
2 Is the car insured if it is stolen?
3 Is the car insured in case I damage it?
4 Do I need extra insurance in case the car is stolen?
5 Will I have to pay any local taxes in local currency?
6 Do I have to collect the car from the car rental office?
7 If I want a child seat, will it cost extra?
8 Is there an extra charge for more than one driver?
9 Can I rent a car if I'm 20 years old?
10 What do I have to show the car hire company when I collect the car?

D Role play

One of you should look at Activity 13 on page 114, the other at Activity 28 on page 122.

You'll be playing the roles of CAR RENTAL CLERK and CLIENT. This role play is in two parts.

A1 Look at the photos. What places are shown, do you think? What are the differences between the traffic in the photos and the traffic in your town or city?

2 You'll hear a British person talking about driving in the USA, and an American talking about driving in Britain. Listen and match the information to the countries.

3 What is the equivalent information about driving in your country?

They drive on the left.
They drive on the right.
Drivers stop at pedestrian crossings to let people cross.
Everyone in the car must wear a seat belt.
Most drivers seem to ignore speed limits.
The speed limit is 30 mph in towns.
The speed limit is 70 mph on motorways/highways.
There are a lot of roundabouts.
There are special lanes for cars carrying passengers.
You can overtake on the inside.
You can turn right at a red traffic light.

B1 Imagine that you're talking to a visitor from the USA who wants to rent a car. What would you say to him/her to explain what these signs mean?

1 2 3 4 5 6 7 8 9 10 11 12

2 Grammar

Write a sentence explaining each sign. Begin your explanations like this:

This sign means that you . . .

and use these verbs:

have to   mustn't   should   shouldn't   can   can't

Welcome to Florida...

Before you proceed with your travel plans, please take a moment to review these important safety tips for Florida visitors. We would like to provide you with a few safety reminders during your stay:

- At the airport or while at our rental car facility, do not leave bags or luggage unattended. On arrival at Dollar, be sure to claim your bags from the bus driver. The rental process only requires the renter and additional drivers (if any) to rent a car, so please assign someone in your party to stay with the bags, if applicable.

- Prior to departure, take the time to know the route to your destination. Our counter personnel will be happy to supply you with a map of the area.

- Place all valuables in trunk or glove compartment and lock. Do not leave valuable items in car if visible to individuals passing by.

- Ask directions only from police or at a well-lit business area or service station. If you need to stop **for any reason**, do so at well-lit or populated areas.

- If your car is malfunctioning, drive to a well-lit area. Call the Dollar Rent A Car location where you rented the car or the emergency road service phone number: **1-800-423-4704**.

- If you are told by passing motorists that something is wrong with your vehicle, **do not** stop. Drive to the nearest service station or populated area.

- Keep doors and windows locked at all times. We recommend that customers driving convertibles keep the top down only during daylight and only after arrival at your hotel or final destination.

- **Do not** pull over to assist what may appear to be a disabled car, even if someone tries to wave you down for help.

- If your vehicle is bumped from behind, **do not** stop until reaching a service station or well-populated area.

- At night, park car in a well-lit area, especially at shopping malls. Check the interior of the vehicle and surrounding areas before entering the vehicle. Be sure to have your keys ready to unlock car doors prior to entering the vehicle. Be sure to have your keys ready to unlock car doors prior to entering a parking lot.

- **Do not** pick up hitch hikers under any circumstances.

- In the event you need police, **call 911**.

- **Do not** stop for flashing white lights or flashing headlights. These are not police procedures. Lights on emergency vehicles are red or red and blue.

- Your car should have a full tank of gas/petrol when you leave the rental facility. Before departing, please ensure this is the case.

- Use seat belts – buckle up (driver and passengers). It is the law and can save lives and reduce serious injuries in the event of an accident.

- Please remember, your personal belongings are not worth physical harm.

Thank you for choosing Dollar Rent A Car. We hope that your stay in Florida is safe and enjoyable!

C Look at the advice to drivers in Florida above. Which of this advice would you also give to motorists in *your* country? Put a tick (✓) beside the advice that is applicable to driving in your country. Put a cross (✗) beside the advice that isn't relevant for your country.

D 1 Role play

Take it in turns to play the roles of a LOCAL RESIDENT and a VISITOR who is going to rent a car in your country.

VISITOR You've never driven in this country before. Ask for advice.
LOCAL RESIDENT What advice are you going to give? Answer the visitor's questions.

> How long will it take to drive to some other cities in the country? How far are some of the tourist attractions?

> Don't forget to ...
> You aren't allowed to ...
> If you drive on the motorway ...

2 Writing

Write a letter to someone who is planning a fly-drive holiday in your country, giving him or her advice on motoring in your country.

TV TOWER

EATON'S
DEPARTMENT
STORE

ODEON
CINEMA

MIDLAND
BANK

SOUTH STREET

BURGER
KING

OLD CITY

McDONALD'S

EL GRECO
RESTAURANT

NORTH STREET

EAST STREET

WEST STREET

CENTRAL AVENUE

ROYAL
HOTEL

BROADWAY

MAIN STREET

A1 You'll hear some guests at the Royal Hotel asking where these places are in the city. Listen and mark where each place is on the street plan.

the railway station City Hall the nearest pharmacy the art gallery

2 What would you say to a guest who wants to get from the Royal Hotel to these places in the city?

Eaton's department store the Odeon cinema the El Greco restaurant McDonald's

B   Role play

💬 👥 One of you should look at Activity 15 on page 115, the other at Activity 31 on page 123.

You'll be playing the roles of RECEPTIONIST and GUEST at the Royal Hotel. This role play is in two parts.

> *Can you tell me where . . . is?*

> *It's on the right.*
> *It's three blocks north of . . .*
> *It's right next door to . . .*
> *It's just around the corner from . . .*
> *It's just opposite McDonald's.*

C 1   👥👥 Think about your own town or city, or the place where you're studying. What would you say to a visitor who asks these questions:

- Where is the best viewpoint to see the town or city from?
- Which is the best hotel? Where is it?
- Where is the best department store?
- Which inexpensive restaurant would you recommend? Where is it?
- Which luxury restaurant would you recommend? Where is it?

2   Note down four places in your town or city which tourists most often go to.

1 ....
2 ....
3 ....
4 ....

3   Role play

👥 Take it in turns to play the roles of a TOURIST in your home town or city and a LOCAL RESIDENT. The local resident is explaining to the tourist how to get to the places you noted down in C2.

> Most people find it hard to understand and remember directions. If possible, show them the route on a street plan. The quickest route isn't always the easiest route to follow. A zig-zag route involving shortcuts is harder to explain and follow than a route where, for example, you go north five blocks and then east four blocks.
>
> You can help people to know they're on the right route if you mention large buildings and places with easy-to-remember names that they will go past.

A1 You'll hear four people describing a problem they had to deal with.
Listen and match the speakers to the problems in the pictures.

 Jim

 Anna

 Tony

 Karen

1

2

3

4

2 Can you guess how each person dealt with each problem?

3 You'll hear how the people dealt with the problems. Listen and find out if
you guessed right. Decide if these statements are true (✓) or false (✗).

1 The guest drove off in his replacement car the same day. ☐
   The police never found the car. ☐

2 Room service had to go out to buy some dog food. ☐
   The chef prepared a special meal for them. ☐

3 The client managed to get seats on another flight. ☐
   The tour operators were unhelpful. ☐

4 The child shared a room at the airport hotel. ☐
   They waited at the airport until the child was collected. ☐

Remember that a visitor may not know
how things work in your country.
As a local person you can help with
problems – or you may know
someone else who can help.

B1 👥 Here are some more problems you might have to deal with. Decide together how you would deal with each of them.

I've locked myself out of my car. The keys are inside and so is my wallet. I'm afraid someone might break into it if I leave it unattended.

I've lost my airline ticket. I'm booked to fly on the 11 a.m. flight to London. It's already 9.30 and I still have to get to the airport.

My car has two flat tyres. I've got to drive to a meeting and I'm due there in an hour.

I've turned on both taps in my bath and I can't turn them off. They are completely stuck and the bath is about to overflow.

My room is on the ground floor and someone keeps looking into my window.

I feel terrible: I've got a terrible headache and I feel sick. I think I've got food poisoning.

2 Role play

👤+👤 Take it in turns to role play each of the situations you discussed in B1.

C Role play

💬 👥 One of you should look at Activity 27 on page 121, the other at Activity 34 on page 124.

You'll be playing the roles of GUEST and MEMBER OF STAFF. The guest will have some more difficulties.

Is there anything I can do?
Would you like me to ...?
What I suggest you do is this: ...

42 Dealing with complaints

A You'll hear five people talking about how they deal with complaints. Listen and match the comments to the people who say them.

1 Complaints give us a chance to prevent the same problem happening again.
2 Clients don't like to feel their complaint has been ignored.
3 Don't take complaints personally. Perhaps ask the duty manager to deal with the situation.
4 People get cross when something goes wrong if they have saved all year for their holiday.
5 The staff of a hotel are a team with shared responsibilities.

waitress

travel agent

receptionist

hotel general manager

restaurant manager

B1 What has happened in the situations below? If you were the person responsible, what would you do? What would you say to each of the guests?

2 You'll hear members of staff dealing with each of the complaints. Listen and decide what each of them did wrong. What *should* they have done and said?

3 You'll hear the same members of staff dealing with the complaints more effectively. Listen and decide why each one is better this time. Did they do what *you* would have done?

C1 Pronunciation

Listen to these sentences and practise saying them in a sincere apologetic voice.

> I'm terribly sorry about that, sir.
> I'm really very sorry about this, madam.
> I'll do it right away, sir.
> I'll see to it right away, madam.
> I'll look into it right away, Mr Brown.
> I'll make sure it doesn't happen again.

2 Here are some things that clients might say to you. Decide together:

● how to deal with each complaint.
● what you will actually say to each client (your exact words).

> My steak is overcooked.
> The heating in my room isn't working.
> The wine waiter was very rude to me when I asked for red wine with my fish.
> You forgot to wake me at 6am. Now I've missed my train.

> There's no hot water in my room.
> The TV in my room only shows two channels and they're both in Hungarian.
> The pool attendant told me I couldn't reserve a sunbed before breakfast.
> The trams going past my room kept me awake all night.

3 Role play

Join a different partner Role play the situations you discussed in C2.
Take it in turns to play the role of the GUEST.

D1 Role play

One of you should look at Activity 12 on page 113, the other at Activity 35 on page 124.

You'll be playing the roles of GUEST and MEMBER OF STAFF. The member of staff will have to deal with some more complaints.

2 Writing

Write a letter to a guest who has written to you to complain about three of the things you dealt with in D1.

> Some complaints may be unreasonable or unjustified, or they may not be your fault. But it's usually best to apologise and offer to take action. In a service industry 'The customer is always right' (even if he or she is wrong). An apology costs nothing and can help the client to feel better. Remember that complaints can help you to improve your service in future.

"You know I must have been mistaken, it tastes fine after all."

A1 Read this advice for tourists. Which are the three most important pieces of advice that you'd give to a visitor to *your* country?

2 👥 What would you say to someone who asked you *why* they should follow each tip?

> *If you answer the door without verifying who it is, you might be letting a criminal into your room.*
> *If you don't use the main entrance late at night . . .*

TRAVELER SAFETY TIPS

1 Don't answer the door in a hotel or motel room without verifying who it is. If a person claims to be an employee, call the front desk and ask if someone from their staff is supposed to have access to your room and for what purpose.

2 When returning to your hotel or motel late in the evening, use the main entrance of the hotel. Be observant and look around before entering parking lots.

3 Close the door securely whenever you are in your room and use all of the locking devices provided.

4 Don't needlessly display guest room keys in public or carelessly leave them on restaurant tables, at the swimming pool, or other places where they can be easily stolen.

5 Do not draw attention to yourself by displaying large amounts of cash or expensive jewelry.

6 Don't invite strangers to your room.

7 Place all valuables in the hotel or motel's safe deposit box.

8 Do not leave valuables in your vehicle.

9 Check to see that any sliding glass doors or windows and any connecting room doors are locked.

10 If you see any suspicious activity, please report your observations to the management.

B1 👥👥👥👥 Discuss these questions about safety and keeping out of trouble:

- Which of the pieces of advice in **A1** is *not* really necessary for your country?
- What parts of your town or city would you advise a tourist to avoid at night? What would you say to them exactly?
- If you're going out or returning home late at night, what precautions do *you* take? Why?

2 Role play

👥👥 **Play the roles of a VISITOR and a LOCAL RESIDENT.**

VISITOR Find out what you should do to avoid risks in the hotel and in the town.
LOCAL RESIDENT Advise the visitor how to avoid risks.

C Writing

Write a handout for visitors to your town or city, advising them about safety.

Dear Visitor

Welcome to ....!

We hope that you will enjoy your stay here, and we would like to suggest some simple precautions you should take to make sure that your stay is safe and pleasant.

1

2

3

4

93

44 Difficult customers?

A1

You'll hear three people talking about how they deal with awkward customers. Listen and decide if these statements are true (✓) or false (✗).

1 **Jane** describes a passenger who refused to stop smoking. ☐
2 The passenger became violent and the crew had to handcuff him. ☐
3 The passenger had to fly home on a Qantas flight. ☐
4 If a special meal isn't available, she tries to make the passenger feel important. ☐

5 **Fiona** describes a party of customers who didn't have a reservation. ☐
6 The customers were rude to her. ☐

7 **Sam** talks about customers who discover they don't like the dish they've ordered. ☐
8 If customers are unfamiliar with Mexican food, they can ask the staff for advice. ☐
9 Sam describes a customer who wanted a Chinese dish. ☐
10 Even at very busy times customers can order variations from the menu. ☐

2

👤👤👤👤 Have you had any similar experiences of difficult clients?
Tell each other what happened and how you dealt with them.

B1

You'll hear eight clients asking you to do something for them. It may be difficult to understand them because they all speak very quickly or unclearly. Listen and tick (✓) the boxes to show what each person wants you to do.

1 Mr Adams wants to reserve a double room …
for 4 nights from 3 July. ☐   for 3 nights from 4 July. ☐

2 Mrs Butler wants someone to move the beds …
together. ☐   apart. ☐

3 Mr Cohen wants you to have his bill ready at …
6am. ☐   6pm. ☐

4 Ms Daniels wants you to phone her office. The number is …
58903, ext 60. ☐   58930, ext 16. ☐

5 Mr Edwards wants you to book …
a table at 8 o'clock for 7 people. ☐   a table at 7 o'clock for 8 people. ☐

6 Mrs Foster wants you to book two tickets for …
the opera house tour. ☐   the opera performance. ☐

7 Mr Graham wants a wake-up call at …
6.15. ☐   6.50. ☐

8 Ms Hughes has two bags. She …
wants someone to help her with them. ☐
doesn't need anyone to help her with them. ☐

> Don't panic if you don't understand what someone says, and don't try to guess what they said. If you're not sure, ask them to repeat what they said. Make sure you understand exactly what they want.

2 Pronunciation

Listen to these phrases and practise saying them politely and clearly.

> I'm sorry, could you say that again more slowly, please?
> I'm sorry, I didn't quite understand what you said.
> I'm sorry, I didn't quite follow what you said.

C Role play

1 Take it in turns to play the roles of a difficult GUEST and a MEMBER OF STAFF. Read each other's information before you begin the role play.

GUEST You are hard to please. You are dissatisfied because:

- You ordered breakfast in your room and they brought you coffee instead of tea.
  The coffee was cold.
  And you ordered it for 8am but they brought it at 7.30.

- Last night the fire alarm rang at midnight. It was a false alarm.
  The fire escape route was locked.
  You had to stand outside the hotel in your pyjamas for half an hour till you were allowed back in.
  Nobody apologised for this at the time.

MEMBER OF STAFF Be prepared for what the guest is going to say by reading the information opposite first.

Remain calm and don't lose your temper. Apologise for each problem.

2 Now change roles.

MEMBER OF STAFF Be prepared for what the guest is going to say by reading the information opposite first.
Remain calm and don't lose your temper. Apologise for each problem.

GUEST You are hard to please. You are dissatisfied because:

- You had to wait 20 minutes for a table in the restaurant.
  They made you sit in a corner near the toilets.
  You had to order from the *à la carte* menu because the main courses on the *table d'hôte* menu weren't available.
  The wine waiter didn't come till you had nearly finished your first course.

- The chambermaid burst into your room and woke you up this morning.
  She didn't come back to make up your room till the afternoon.
  She didn't clean the bathroom properly.
  The housekeeper was unhelpful when you told her about this.

"The complaints against you are as follows: You don't return calls, you don't encourage your staff, and you're nobody's best friend."

A 👥👥👥👥 Look at the photos and discuss these questions:

- Where are the places shown in the photos?
- Put them in order: which would you most like to visit? Why?
- What kind of places do you like to visit on holiday (or at the weekend)?
- Why is it that people like to go sightseeing when they're on holiday?

B1 👥👥 Explain the difference between each of these pairs of sights and attractions:

art gallery ↔ historical museum   mountain ↔ hill
theme park ↔ national park   monument ↔ viewpoint
castle ↔ old city   market ↔ shopping centre

> *An art gallery shows paintings and sculptures.*
> *A historical museum tells you about the history of the area or city.*

2 Vocabulary *Describing*

Choose two words and phrases from the list below that you *can* use to describe each of the attractions in B1 to a client, and one that you would *not* use.

interesting   fascinating   enjoyable   unusual   worth visiting
worth the trip   attractive   superb   wonderful   nice   lovely
charming   impressive   unforgettable   beautiful   pretty
rewarding   tiring   large   dull   high   exhausting   worthwhile

> *The National Gallery is worth visiting: it's fascinating.*
> [not *attractive*]
> *Mount Fuji is wonderful: it's very impressive.*
> [not *fascinating*]

Futuroscope

C1

You'll hear three people answering this question:

What is the number one tourist attraction in your city or region?

Listen and match the places to the reasons 1–6 why tourists find each one popular.

1 It's a great place for walking.
2 It's very different from what you'd expect.
3 You can learn about famous film directors.
4 You can swim in the lakes.
5 You get a very full day of entertainment.
6 You learn about English history.

Royal Pavilion

2

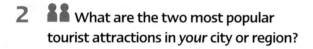 What are the two most popular tourist attractions in *your* city or region?

....

....

Note down what you would tell a visitor about both of the attractions.

1 Why are they popular?
2 What kind of people enjoy them most?
3 What are the opening times?
4 What's the best time to go to avoid the crowds?
5 How do you get there by car?
6 How do you get there by public transport?

Write down *three* more questions that people might ask you about them.

The Lake District

3 Role play

Join a different partner Imagine that one of you is a foreign TOURIST. Role play a conversation about *one* of the attractions you discussed in C2. Use the words and phrases from B2. Then change roles and talk about a different attraction.

> You'd enjoy a visit to . . .
> because . . .
> While you're here why don't
> you go to . . . ?
> If you want to go to . . . the
> best time to go is . . .

4 Writing

Write a letter to a person who is going to stay in your city or region, explaining what there is to do in the area during their holiday.

Making suggestions and giving advice

A1 What kind of weather is shown in the pictures? What would you say to a visitor if each kind of weather was expected today?
Begin like this: *It's going to . . .*

2 You'll hear five weather forecasts. Listen and match the descriptions of the weather to the dates.

March 1st	sunny and warm all day
April 1st	sunshine and showers
May 1st	thunderstorms in the afternoon
June 1st	heavy rain later
July 1st	sunny but very cold all day

3 What advice would you give to each of these clients, if they were dressed like this on the days shown?

March 1	April 1	May 1	June 1	July 1

> *It might be a good idea to . . .*
> *I think it would be better to . . .*
> *I think you should perhaps . . .*
> *I don't think you need to . . .*
> *It might be better not to . . .*
> *I don't think you should . . .*

4 Role play

👥 Take it in turns to play the roles of the CLIENTS in the pictures and a MEMBER OF STAFF. Begin each conversation by saying '*Good morning*' and then use the phrases in the speech balloon.

> People from other countries may be surprised by the weather in your country, and they may find it hard to get used to. They may not know what kind of clothes to wear, or if they should take extra warm clothes with them on a day trip. You may need to advise them.

B1   🯁🯁 **Discuss these questions:**

- During which months (if ever) are the weather conditions in the list most likely in your region?

  sunny hot snowing foggy raining cold cloudy fine windy

- What could a tourist do in such weather?

2 Role play

Join a different partner Take it in turns to play the roles of a GUEST and a RECEPTIONIST. Use the useful phrases in the speech balloon as you talk about what the guest could do this weekend in the different kinds of weather you discussed in B1.

> *What do you think I should do if it's . . . this weekend?*

> *If it's . . . you could . . .*
> *Well, if it's . . . you won't be able to . . . So why don't you . . . ?*
> *If it's . . . the best thing to do is . . .*
> *If it's . . . the only thing you can do is . . .*

C1   🯁🯁 If a visitor asked you for advice on these topics about your own town or city, what advice would you give? What would you say to the visitor?

I want to go to the countryside, the mountains and the coast. Should I drive or take the train?
I want to do some shopping for clothes.
Is there a good night club?

2 Role play

🯁🯁 One of you should look at Activity 16 on page 115, the other at Activity 29 on page 122.

You'll be asking for and giving more advice about your own town or city and playing the roles of GUEST and RECEPTIONIST. This role play is in two parts.

> Because of your professional knowledge and because you know about your own region, clients will often ask you for your advice. But make sure that it's clear from your tone of voice that you're making a suggestion, not giving them an order.

A1 Find the answers to these questions in the advertisement:

- How many attractions that begin with the letter *s* are mentioned?
- What other attractions *not* beginning with the letter *s* are mentioned?

Sun, Sea, Sand, Summer, Spain

IT'S NO COINCIDENCE that so many people's idea of an ideal holiday starts with the same letter. Over the years, the beach holiday has become synonymous with *Spain*. And rightly so. In *Spain*, you can still enjoy all the fun of the fair without your beach towel. Of course, should you tire of soaking up the sun lying down, you can always soak up the sea in a variety of other positions. For the energetic, most Spanish resorts offer every watersport under the sun (and several under the sea). And for the less energetic a cool glass of sangria (there's that letter again) is normally within easy reach. When the Spanish sun reluctantly dips below the horizon, the nightlife lights up the night and continues to do so until the sun makes a reappearance. At the end of the holiday, you'll begin to understand why the natives occasionally feel the need for another word beginning with a sibilant sound. *Siesta*.

For further information please contact your travel agent. The Spanish Tourist Office, 57 St. James's Street, London SW1A 1LD

2 You'll hear three people who have visited different parts of Spain. Listen and tick (✓) the boxes to show the reasons why they enjoyed their visits.

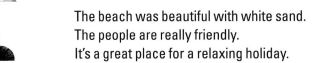

It used to be very unspoilt. ☐
There are lots of parks to walk in. ☐
The food is delicious. ☐

The weather is hot and sunny. ☐
The nightlife is brilliant. ☐
You can get everywhere easily by public transport. ☐

The beach was beautiful with white sand. ☐
The people are really friendly. ☐
It's a great place for a relaxing holiday. ☐

3 👥 Why do tourists come to visit *your* region (or country)? Make a list of the main reasons.

4 *Join another pair* Compare your lists and discuss these questions:

● What are the *four* most important reasons you've listed?

● Why are visitors sometimes disappointed when they visit your region (or country)? What might discourage them from coming again?

● What is your own idea of an ideal holiday destination? Where would you go if you could afford it, and what would you do there?

B1 Vocabulary *Adjectives*

Decide which of these adjectives you would use in a holiday advertisement or brochure.

attractive beautiful cloudy crowded delicious delightful depressing dusty exciting fertile hospitable relaxing refreshing remote sunny warm

2 Read the advertisement for Thailand. Which of the attractions would apply to your own region (or country)?

3 Writing

Write an advertisement for your own region (or country).

Fun & sun in THAILAND

Southern Thailand offers beautiful sunshine in equal measure. And while it's wonderful to stretch out on a deserted beach, there are plenty of other options to fill your time with. Take a boat trip to our outlying islands; submerge yourself in our spectacular coral reefs or go exploring in pristine rainforests. And, when you're ready for refreshment, enjoy fresh, succulent seafood straight from the sea. with convenient flights from all over Asia to Bangkok, and easy connections to Phuket and Krabi, a rejuvenating adventure in southern Thailand is a lot closer than you might think. THAI, smooth as silk.

A1 You'll hear four tourists asking about the banknotes you can see in the pictures. Listen and fill the blanks in these sentences:

1 Michael Faraday is famous for his experiments with .... and
....

2 Clara Schumann was the .... of Robert Schumann and a famous
.... in her own right.

3 Natsume Soseki was a famous Japanese .... His most famous novel
Kokoro (which means the ....) is very sad.

4 George Washington was the .... US president. He commanded the American
army in the war of .... and defeated the British army at Yorktown.

2 Have a look at the banknotes in your own wallets (and any coins which have portraits on them). Discuss these questions:

● What would you say to a visitor who asks you about each person on the banknotes (and coins)?

● Who are the *five* most famous historical figures in your country's history? What would you say about them to a visitor who has never heard of any of them?

● Whose statues can visitors see in the main square of your town or city? What are the people famous for?

B1 Read the brief history of Mexico opposite and find the answers to these questions:

1 Who was Moctezuma II?
2 How many men did Cortés have?
3 For how long was Mexico a Spanish colony?
4 Which states of the USA used to be part of Mexico?
5 Who was Maximilian?

2 Discuss these questions:

● What are the three most important dates in your country's history?
● What would you say to a visitor about them?

A brief history of Mexico

Ancient Mexico was the home of three major cultures: the Olmecs from 1500 to 600 BC, the Mayans whose civilization was most developed in the 6th century AD, and the Aztecs. The Aztecs founded a fine modern city in 1325 at Tenochtitlán: it had spring water and pyramids where human sacrifices were performed.

In 1519, the Spanish general Hernán Cortés and 600 men landed at Veracruz and marched to Tenochtitlán. They made the Aztec emperor Moctezuma II a prisoner and took over the city. But the Indians fought back and drove the Spanish out. Two years later the Spanish defeated the Aztecs and destroyed the city. It was rebuilt as Mexico City, the capital of New Spain. Within ten years many of the Indians had been converted to Christianity, but they were treated very much as slaves by the Spanish.

Mexico was ruled by Spain until 1821 when it became independent. In 1847 the US army invaded Mexico and defeated the Mexican Army. The states of California, New Mexico, Arizona and Texas became part of the USA after this.

After a devastating civil war, Benito Juárez, a Zapotec Indian, became president in 1861 and he introduced many reforms. In 1863 Napoleon III's French army entered Mexico City and the Austrian Maximilian became emperor of Mexico. A republican force under Porfirio Díaz eventually reconquered the country in 1867 and Juárez became president again. Díaz himself was president-dictator from 1877 to 1911.

In 1917, after a period of guerrilla fighting, led by Emiliano Zapata and Pancho Villa, a new liberal constitution was drawn up. Venustiano Carranza became president as leader of the Revolutionary Party.

C **Look at the photos and discuss these questions:**

- What's happening in each of these pictures?
- What would you say to a visitor who asks you these questions:

  Where can I go to see local dancing?

  Where can I buy local handicrafts?

  Where can I go to find out about local folklore and local history?

49 A nice day out

A 1 Read the extracts opposite from a guide book. If you had a free afternoon in Paris, and you only had time to go to *one* place, which would you visit? Why?

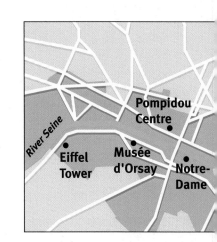

2 Answer these tourists' questions about the places:

1 Is Tuesday evening a good time to go to the Pompidou Centre?
2 Is there a nice restaurant in the Pompidou Centre?
3 Where's the best place to see paintings by Picasso?
4 Where are the Impressionist paintings?
5 What kind of building is the Musée d'Orsay?
6 What's the best time to go up the Tower of Notre-Dame?
7 Where can I board a boat cruise on the River Seine?
8 Can I enjoy the view from the top floor of the Eiffel Tower in the evening?
9 How long does it take to get to the top of the Eiffel Tower?
10 What else is there to do near the Eiffel Tower?

B 👥 Make a list of *four* of the most popular tourist attractions in your own region. Then discuss these questions:

● What does each have to offer?
● What *less* popular places would you recommend to a visitor who wants to experience your region and its culture?

C 1 👥👥 Devise a recommended day out (by car or by public transport) for tourists visiting your city/region. Include some *unusual* places which tourists don't usually visit.

2 Role play

👥👥+👥👥 Take it in turns to describe your day out to the other group. Imagine that they are visitors and they have asked you to suggest a day's excursion to them.

D Writing

Write a one-page handout describing your recommended day out, including a paragraph about each place that will be visited.

A day out by car

If you have a day to spare, and you'd like to find out more about this region, you might like to try this outing.

MUSÉE D'ORSAY

This wonderful museum was opened in 1986. It displays works of art from the second half of the 19th century (1848–1910). The original building designed by Victor Laloux was a railway station, which was no longer used. Rather than demolish it, the French government decided to restore the exterior and alter the interior to accommodate paintings and sculptures in an unusual and impressive setting.

MUST SEE:
- *Paintings by the French Impressionists, including famous works by: Vincent Van Gogh, Pierre-Auguste Renoir, Claude Monet, Edgar Degas and Paul Cézanne.*
- *Edouard Manet's* Le Déjeuner sur l'Herbe, *showing a group of artists and young women having a picnic in a forest.*

OPENING TIMES
April–Oct 09:00–18:00
Nov–Mar 10:00–18:00
Sundays 09:00–18:00
Closed Mondays
– the best time to visit is early on a weekday or on Thursday evening (open till 21:45)

While you're in the area …
- Cross the river by the footbridge and walk upstream along the bank of the Seine towards Notre-Dame. If you make a short detour, you will be able to see Claude Monet's famous paintings of water lilies, which are displayed in the Orangerie Museum.

POMPIDOU CENTRE

Parisians call this amazing building the *Beaubourg*. It was designed by Renzo Piano, Richard Rogers and Gianfranco Franchini and opened in 1977. The building is like an inside-outside building, with all the pipes, lifts and escalators on the outside – green water pipes, yellow electricity cables, blue ventilation tubes, red escalators, lifts and walkways.

At the front of the building is a huge piazza where you can enjoy street performers. The building contains a museum,

a library, exhibition areas and an unpretentious restaurant, which has a lovely view over the old buildings of the area.

MUST SEE:
- *National Museum of Modern Art on the 5th floor. This museum has 30,000 works of art but only 800 on display at any one time. Works by Henri Matisse, Joan Miró, René Magritte, Salvador Dali – and an ever-changing display of surprising controversial modern art from Europe and America.*

OPENING TIMES (MUSEUM)
Mon, Wed–Fri noon–22:00,
Sat–Sun 10:00–22:00
Closed Tuesdays
– the best time to visit is in the evening

While you're in the area …
- Take a stroll around the area to see the historic buildings, and have a drink in one of the pavement cafés and watch the people walking past.
- Visit the Picasso Museum nearby, which has an impressive display of works by Pablo Picasso housed in an old palace.

NOTRE-DAME CATHEDRAL

This Gothic cathedral was built in the heart of Paris between 1163 and 1330, on the site of a Roman temple. It dominates the Île de la Cité, the island in the River Seine from which Paris expanded over the centuries. There are 387 steps to the top of the tower, but the climb is worth it.

MUST SEE:
- *The interior, including the three beautiful rose windows.*
- *The view from the tower (and the famous gargoyles at the top).*

OPENING TIMES
Cathedral: 08:00–19:00
Tower: 10:00–17:00
– the best time for a visit is early in the morning

While you're in the area …
- Allow yourself plenty of time to stroll around Île de la Cité and Île St Louis to see the historic buildings, squares and gardens.
- Walk around the island on the bank of the river.
- Take a river cruise from near the Pont Neuf (the oldest and longest bridge in Paris).

EIFFEL TOWER

The Eiffel Tower is the symbol of Paris but when it was built for the Universal Exhibition in 1889, it was meant to be a temporary building. It was designed by the engineer Gustave Eiffel. It was the world's tallest building until the Empire State Building was completed in New York in 1932.

There are lifts to take visitors to each of three levels, but if you feel energetic you can take the stairs to the First level (360 steps), Second level (700 steps) or even the Third level (1652 steps). At busy times it may take 2 hours to reach the top by lift because of the queues.

One of the best restaurants in Paris is the Jules Verne Restaurant (Second level), where you can enjoy panoramic views and eat excellent food.

MUST SEE:
- *Cinémax museum – interesting film showing the history of the Tower and famous people visiting it, including Adolf Hitler and Charlie Chaplin.*
- *The view from the Third level (274m high).*

OPENING TIMES
Apr–Oct 09:00–23:00 (to midnight in July & August)
Nov–Mar 09:30–23:00
– the best times to go up are early in the morning and before sunset

While you're in the area …
- Walk along the river to Les Invalides to see the Dôme Church and the tomb of Napoléon Bonaparte.
- Also visit the Rodin Museum nearby, which displays famous sculptures by Auguste Rodin including *The Thinker* and *The Kiss.*

50 The future of tourism

A1 You'll hear a discussion about the pros and cons of tourism. Listen and fill the blanks in this summary of what is said:

Advantages

1 Tourism is an important source of .... for local people.
2 Tourism benefits the .... of a country or region.
3 Foreign .... comes into the country.
4 Local .... and .... earn money by selling food to hotels.
5 Taxes raised from tourism improve life for .... in the country.

Disadvantages

1 Work in the tourism industry doesn't offer much ....
2 The benefits of tourism aren't always felt at a .... level.
3 The profits from hotels may not stay in the .... or ....
4 Many hotels prefer to import food from ....
5 The relative prosperity of tourists may encourage ....

2 **Discuss these questions:**

● What are the advantages and disadvantages of tourism in *your* region?
● Which of the points made in the broadcast are most relevant to your country?
● In general, how well do tourists in your country behave?

B1 Look at this advice to tourists. Which of the tips are Dos and which are Don'ts? Fill the blanks with Do or Don't.

2 Which of the tips do you disagree with? Why?

How to be a responsible tourist

● .... waste water. Tourists place a great strain on the local water supply.

● .... stick to marked paths when walking in the countryside and .... damage any plants.

● .... pick flowers – leave them for others to enjoy.

● .... take care with cigarette ends and matches.

● .... have your picture taken with wild animals used by photographers.

● .... turn off the lights when you leave your room.

● .... buy local products and services rather than imported goods, foods and drinks.

● .... buy souvenirs that might put at risk endangered species or the natural environment. Avoid animal skins, ivory, rare flowers, mounted butterflies, shells, turtle products and rare flowers.

● .... try to stay in locally-owned hotels, rather than multinationals where little of the money you spend remains in the country.

● .... follow the Green Tourist Code: "Take only photos, leave only footprints, kill only time" – but .... ask people's permission before you take their photos, and .... leave too many footprints!

C1 👥 Look at these pictures showing tourists behaving badly. What are they doing? Which of the behaviour do you think is the worst? And which is the least bad?

2 Writing

Write '10 Tips' to encourage visitors to your country to behave responsibly. Refer to the tips in B1 and the pictures above, and perhaps add some points of your own.

Communication activities

1 In these six short role plays you'll be playing the role of guest or member of staff — or observer. The observer listens to the role play and then gives the others feedback on how polite and friendly they sounded.

1 You are a GUEST. Find out where the nearest toilet is. Start by saying 'Good morning'.

2 You are a MEMBER OF STAFF. Explain that there is a bus to the city centre from the bus stop opposite (tickets cost 80 cents). Or a taxi would cost about $5.

3 You are the OBSERVER. Listen to your partners. Tell them how polite, helpful and friendly they sound. If they sound cold or rude, ask them to do the role play again.

4 You are a GUEST. Find out where you can get a good local meal.

5 You are a MEMBER OF STAFF. Explain that there is a kiosk just round the corner. They have postcards and stamps. A stamp for a postcard abroad costs 50 cents.

6 You are the OBSERVER. Listen to your partners. If they sound cold or rude, ask them to do the role play again.

2 This role play is in two parts so that you both get a turn at being the travel agent.

1 You are a CLIENT. The travel agent will show you your itinerary (in Activity 18). Ask the travel agent to explain it to you. (There's one mistake in the itinerary.)

2 You are the TRAVEL AGENT. Explain this itinerary to the client, but first read it through to make sure that you understand it!

Your Itinerary

date	flight no.	from	dep	to	arr	check in
1 March	SR 410	Zurich	0730	Seattle/Tacoma	0135	Terminal A 0640
6 March	AA 524	Seattle/Tacoma	1159			1055
7 March				Dallas/Fort Worth	0546	
7 March	AA 1341	Dallas/Fort Worth	0650	Guadalajara	0918	
9 March	AA 1908	Guadalajara	1000	Los Angeles	1113	0900
19 March	SR 109	Los Angeles	0850			International Terminal 1950
20 March				Zurich	1604	

3 This role play is in two parts, so that you both get a turn at being the member of staff.

1 You are a MEMBER OF STAFF. Interview the guest to find out his/her answers to the questions on this customer survey. Begin like this:

Would you mind helping us by answering a few questions? It won't take very long.

RESERVATIONS
Was your reservation handled courteously and efficiently?   YES ☐   NO ☐
If "No", please tell us how we can improve.
Why did you choose this hotel?

RECEPTION AND SERVICE
Did you receive efficient, friendly and prompt service from:

	Excellent	Good	Satisfactory	Fair	Poor
Doorman	☐	☐	☐	☐	☐
Concierge/Hall porter	☐	☐	☐	☐	☐
Check-in/Guest service	☐	☐	☐	☐	☐
Telephone operator	☐	☐	☐	☐	☐
Maid	☐	☐	☐	☐	☐
Laundry service	☐	☐	☐	☐	☐
Assistant manager	☐	☐	☐	☐	☐
Check-out/Cashier	☐	☐	☐	☐	☐
Overall, I thought the service from the staff was:	☐	☐	☐	☐	☐

Comments: ....

WILL YOU RETURN?
If your travel plans bring you back here, will you return to this hotel?

Definitely	Probably	Maybe	Never	Not Applicable
☐	☐	☐	☐	☐

Why/Why not? ....

Thank you for your time and your co-operation! Thank you for staying with us.

---

2 You are the GUEST. Answer the questions you're asked about the hotel. Use your imagination to think of suitable replies.

4 This role play is in two parts so that you both get a turn at being the receptionist. Today is Sunday, May 1st.

1 You are a RECEPTIONIST at the Royal Hotel. Welcome the guest and go through the check-in procedure. Consult the room chart on page 56.

2 You are MR or MRS GREEN and you're checking in at the Royal Hotel. You sent a fax reserving a room till May 5th. You now want to stay until the 6th — is the room available for an extra night?

5 This role play is in two parts so that you both get a turn at being the travel agent.

1 You are a CLIENT. You want to book a holiday. These are your requirements and details:

> Departure date 23 April
> from London, Gatwick to Orlando, Florida
> arriving there same day
>
> Mr Alan Johnston and Ms Karen O'Neill
> 31 Westerfield Road
> Ipswich IP3 2SN
> home phone 01473 255512   office phone 0171 234 9672
>
> 13 nights accommodation at Suncrest Plaza Hotel, Cocoa Beach
> One double room with balcony and sea view

2 You are the TRAVEL AGENT. Fill out the booking form on page 21 with the information that the client gives you. Finish by phoning the tour operator to check availability.

6 Here are half of the answers to the airport codes quiz. Your partner has the rest of the answers. Which of the answers did you get right? Which couldn't you guess?

ATH	= Athens	LIS	= Lisbon
BUD	= Budapest	MAD	= Madrid
CDG *or* ORY	= Paris (Charles de Gaulle *or* Orly)	MEX	= Mexico City
FRA	= Frankfurt	NRT	= Tokyo (Narita)
HKG	= Hong Kong	PEK	= Beijing
JFK *or* EWR *or* LGA	= New York (JFK, Newark *or* La Guardia)	SYD	= Sydney
		ZRH	= Zurich
LAX	= Los Angeles		

> HKG is Hong Kong — I thought so. I didn't realise that PEK was Beijing.

7 This role play is in four parts so that you both get two turns at filling in the room chart.

1 Your name is BERNARD BROWN. Call the Royal Hotel. You want to reserve a room for your wife and yourself from May 2 to May 6 (four nights). The room must have a bath and balcony. (Your home phone number is 01303 87 92 31.)

2 You are the RESERVATIONS MANAGER at the Royal Hotel. Answer the phone and take the booking. Fill in the room chart on page 56.

3 Your name is CARLOS CHAVEZ. Call the hotel to reserve a single room from May 1 to May 8. (Your office phone number is 0171 993 3723.)

4 You are the RESERVATIONS MANAGER. Take the booking and fill out the room chart on page 56.

8 This role play is in two parts so that you both get a turn at answering enquiries. You'll need to spell some of the difficult names aloud to your partner and say the numbers slowly and clearly.

1 You are a TOURIST. Call the New Zealand Lodge Association and find out the phone numbers for these places:

Moonlight Lodge in Murchison ....

Grasmere Lodge in Christchurch ....

Motueka River Lodge ....

Sherwood Lodge in North Canterbury ....

and the full addresses for these places:

Braemar Lodge in North Canterbury ....

Stewart Island Lodge ....

Lake Brunner Lodge in Westland ....

Remarkables Lodge in Queenstown ....

2 Change roles. Now you are the INFORMATION OFFICER. Refer to this information to answer your client's questions.

LODGE CONTACT DETAILS
North Island

Kingfish Lodge, RD 1, Whangaroa Harbour, Northland, New Zealand.
Tel 64-9-405 0164, fax 64-9-405 0163.

Okiato Lodge, Okiato Point, RD 1, Russell, New Zealand.
Tel 64-9-403 7948, fax 64-9-403 7515.

Inverness Estate, Ness Valley Road, RD 5, Papakura, New Zealand.
Tel 64-9-292 8710, fax 64-9-292 8714.

Fantail Lodge, Rea Road, RD 2, Katikati, New Zealand.
Tel 64-7-549 1581, fax 64-7-549 1417.

Brooklands Country Estate, RD 1, Ngaruawahia, Waikato, New Zealand.
Tel 64-7-825 4756, fax 64-7-825 4873.

Cassimir, RD 3, Tauranga, New Zealand.
Tel 64-7-578 5494, fax 64-7-543 1999.

Moose Lodge, RD 4, Rotorua, Lake Rotoiti, New Zealand.
Tel 64-7-362 7823, fax 64-7-362 7677.

Muriaroha Lodge, 411 Old Taupo Road, PO Box 43, Rotorua, New Zealand.
Tel 64-7-346 1220, fax 64-7-346 1338.

Huka Lodge, Huka Falls Road, PO Box 95, Taupo, New Zealand.
Tel 64-7-378 5791, fax 64-7-378 0427.

Lake Taupo Lodge, PO Box 83, Taupo, New Zealand.
Tel 64-7-378 7386, fax 64-7-377 3226.

Mangapapa Lodge, 466 Napier Road, Havelock North, Hawke's Bay, New Zealand.
Tel 64-6-878 3234, fax 64-6-878 1214.

9 This role play is in four parts so that you both get two turns at noting down messages.

1 You are a CALLER. Leave this message for Arthur Brown, who is a guest at the Bay View Hotel:

> Your name is **Alex McIntosh**. Your phone number is **01423 539435**. You were going to meet Mr Brown at **7.30** at the **Harbour View Restaurant**. You're going to be delayed and now you won't be there till **8.30**. You have phoned the restaurant to change the booking.

2 You are the RECEPTIONIST. Take down the message you're given on one of the message pads on page 35. Check that you have noted down all the information correctly.

3 Now you are the CALLER again. Leave this message for Imogen Christie, who is a guest at the Bay View Hotel:

> Your name is **Sandy Hill**. Your phone number is **01832 973922**. Can Ms Christie make her own way to the meeting tomorrow morning? She can take a taxi. The meeting is at **Janus House, 100 Ocean Boulevard**. If there's any problem, could she phone you?

4 You are the RECEPTIONIST. Take down the message you're given on the other message pad on page 35. Check that you have noted down the information correctly.

10 This role play is in two parts so that you both get a turn at being the waiter/waitress.

1 You are a GUEST. You've finished your coffee. Ask the waiter/waitress to bring you your bill. Listen carefully and make sure he or she gets everything right — especially the arithmetic.

2 You are the WAITER/WAITRESS. Add up the bill in the presence of the guest, checking each item as you go through the order. (Make at least one deliberate mistake!)

Table 30			Total
2	Soup of the day	@ $2.50	
1	Shrimp cocktail	@ $3.00	
1	Fillet steak	@ $18.50	
1	Lobster	@ $24.50	
1	Omelette	@ $9.50	
2	Fresh fruit salad	@ $4.50	
1	Banana split	@ $5.50	
1	bottle of house red	@ $12.00	
1	bottle of mineral water	@ $7.50	
3	cover charge	@ $2.50	
	+ service @ 10%		
		Total =	

> So that's two soups — that's five dollars. And one shrimp cocktail — that's another three dollars.
> Then you had one fillet steak — that's...

11

This role play is in four parts. In the first two parts you are one of the receptionists and different guests will approach you with questions.

1 & 2   You are a RECEPTIONIST on duty at the reception desk at the Hotel Miramar. Answer your guest's queries.

•HOTEL•
MIRAMAR INFORMATION

Rooms with a sea view are $125, rooms overlooking the garden are $99. You have only one $125 room available now, but several for next month.

You can reserve rooms at **associate hotels** in Granada and Mendoza through the computer.

Breakfast is served 6.30–10am in the Atlantic Restaurant on the second floor up the stairs (i.e. first floor for Europeans).

Checking out time is 11am. Luggage can be stored for guests who have checked out.

International flights depart from Simón Bolívar Airport (25km from here). Allow 1 hour by taxi + 1 hour to check in.

Domestic flights depart from National Airport (5 km from here) to other cities:

Mendoza: 8.30 14.30

Granada: 10.30 17.30

Rio Verde: 12.00 18.15.

Allow 30 minutes by taxi + 45 minutes to check in.

There is a comfortable overnight **train** with sleeping cars to Granada, departing at 11pm.

3   You are a GUEST at the Hotel Miramar. Ask one of the receptionists to help you with these questions. Here are the things you want to do . . .

find out about flights to Rio Verde in the south.

change $100 into pesos.

find out what time dinner is served in the hotel.

4   Now ask a *different* receptionist to help you with these questions. You want to . . .

find out when you should leave the hotel for the midnight flight to Miami. Where can you leave your luggage till then?

book a taxi for 8am tomorrow to the university.

go for a swim.

12

Take it in turns to play the roles of guest and member of staff. Keep changing roles. First, you are a guest.

GUEST Make each of these complaints to the member of staff.

1 There seems to be something strange in my soup.

2 I've been waiting a very long time for someone to bring me my bill.

3 The fridge in my room isn't working and it's leaking all over the carpet.

4 I left my Walkman in my room while I was out. When I got back it was lying on the floor, broken.

5 Somebody came to my room this morning and tried to sell me something.

6 You recommended the sightseeing tour to me but it was a waste of time.

MEMBER OF STAFF Deal with the complaints politely and apologetically.

13 This role play is in two parts so that you both get a turn at being the rental clerk.

1 You are a CLIENT. You want to rent a Group B car at this location. You want to have the car now and you'll return it here at the same time one week from now. Find out how much this will cost with unlimited mileage without full insurance.
Begin by saying: *Hello. I'd like to rent a car please.*

2 You are the Car rental clerk. Refer to this information and fill out the form below for the client.

Cars available today: Group A (no cars available); Group B ($120 per week) Nissan Micra;
Group C ($155 per week) Toyota Carina.
Prices include unlimited mileage.
Full insurance: $10 per day
Return to another location: $21 surcharge

Name . . . .
       title   *first name*   *family name*

Car required: Group . . . . Make . . . .

Full insurance required?   Yes ☐   No ☐

Unlimited mileage?   Yes ☐   No ☐

From . . . .
      time   *day*   *month*   *year*

To . . . .
      time   *day*   *month*   *year*

Pick-up location . . . .

Return location . . . .

14 This role play is in two parts so that you both get a turn at being the cashier.

1 You are a CASHIER. Explain to the client how much he or she has to pay.

2 You are the CLIENT. Imagine that you don't trust the cashier's arithmetic. Write down the prices the cashier tells you — and make sure he or she gets the final total right.

Two nights accommodation @ $44 per night	= ☐
Three dinners @ $24 each	= ☐
Four bottles of wine @ $12.50 each	= ☐
Five local telephone calls @ 50¢ each	= ☐
Six glasses of beer @ $3.40 each	= ☐
TOTAL	= ☐

15

1. This role play is in two parts so that you both get a turn at playing each role.

1 You are a GUEST at the Royal Hotel. Ask the receptionist where four of these places are and mark them on the map on page 86.

the Metro cinema	the market	the airline terminal
the Sheraton Hotel	the St Tropez restaurant	the La Lupa restaurant

2 You are a RECEPTIONIST at the Royal Hotel. Explain to the guest how to get to the places marked on this map of the south of the city.

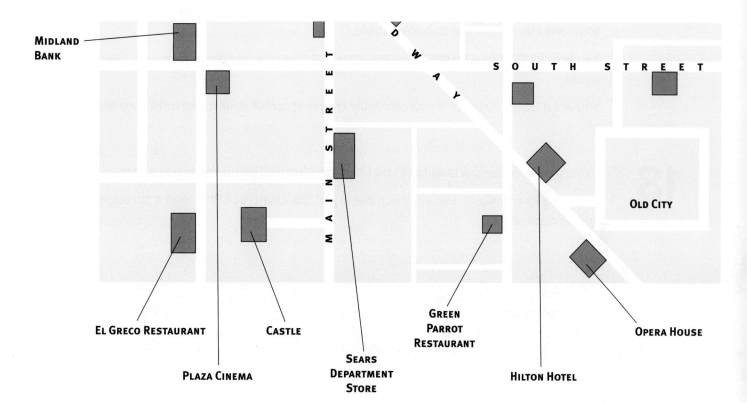

16

This role play is in two parts so that you both get a turn at playing each role.

1 You are a RECEPTIONIST. The guest will ask you for some advice.

2 You are the GUEST. Ask the receptionist these questions:

Can you recommend an inexpensive restaurant?

Is there an art gallery here?

What's the best place to go jogging?

Is there a good bookshop in town?

Can you recommend somewhere for a quick snack?

17

In these six short role plays you'll be playing the role of guest or member of staff — or observer. The observer listens to the role play and then gives the others feedback on how polite and friendly they sounded.

1 You are a MEMBER OF STAFF. Explain that the toilets are down the stairs on the right.

2 You are the OBSERVER. Listen to your partners. Tell them how polite, helpful and friendly they sound. If they sound cold or rude, ask them to do the role play again.

3 You are a GUEST. Find out what the dialling code for a phone call to the UK is.

4 You are a MEMBER OF STAFF. Explain that there is a nice family restaurant two blocks from here. Offer to phone the restaurant to book a table.

5 You are the OBSERVER. Listen to your partners. If they sound cold or rude, ask them to do the role play again.

6 You are a GUEST. Find out if you can delay checking out of your room until 4pm tomorrow.

18

This role play is in two parts so that you both get a turn at being the travel agent.

1 You are a TRAVEL AGENT. Explain this itinerary to the client, but first read it through to make sure that you understand it!

Your Itinerary

date	flight no.	from	dep	to	arr	check in
1 MAY	RO 261	Budapest Ferihegy	0715	Istanbul	0815	Terminal 1 0615
4 MAY	TK 806	Istanbul	0920	Cairo	1140	International Terminal 0820
8 MAY	OS 388	Cairo	1220	Vienna	1655	Terminal 2 1050
8 MAY	OS 295	Vienna	1835	Venice	2005	
12 MAY	OS 294	Venice	0905	Vienna	1035	0805
12 MAY	OS 803	Venice	1140	Budapest	1240	

2 You are the CLIENT. The travel agent will show you your itinerary (in Activity 2). Ask the travel agent to explain it to you. (There's one mistake in the itinerary.)

19 This role play is in two parts so that you both get a turn at being the member of staff.

1 You are a GUEST. Answer the questions you're asked about the hotel. Use your imagination to think of suitable replies.

2 You are a MEMBER OF STAFF. Interview the guest to find out his/her answers to the questions on this customer survey. Begin like this:

Would you mind helping us by answering a few questions? It won't take very long.

RESTAURANT AND BARS

Was the food and beverage quality and service acceptable?

	Excellent	Good	Satisfactory	Fair	Poor
Room service	☐	☐	☐	☐	☐
Restaurant – breakfast	☐	☐	☐	☐	☐
Restaurant – lunch	☐	☐	☐	☐	☐
Restaurant – dinner	☐	☐	☐	☐	☐
Lobby lounge	☐	☐	☐	☐	☐
Poolside snack bar	☐	☐	☐	☐	☐
Night club	☐	☐	☐	☐	☐
Hotel bar	☐	☐	☐	☐	☐

Do you feel that our food and beverage pricing represents good value?   YES ☐   NO ☐

Comments: ....

....

....

Is there something about our restaurants/lounges that you would like to see added, corrected or changed?

GUEST ROOM

Room number .... Dates of stay ....

	Excellent	Good	Satisfactory	Fair	Poor
Cleanliness	☐	☐	☐	☐	☐
Comfort	☐	☐	☐	☐	☐
Equipment	☐	☐	☐	☐	☐
Furnishings	☐	☐	☐	☐	☐
Lighting	☐	☐	☐	☐	☐

Comments: ....

....

....

Is there something about your room that you would like to see added, corrected or changed?

Thank you for your time and your co-operation! Thank you for staying with us.

20   This role play is in two parts so that you both get a turn at being the travel agent.

1   You are a TRAVEL AGENT. Fill out the booking form on page 21 with the information that the client gives you. Finish by phoning the tour operator to check availability.

2   You are the CLIENT. You want to book a holiday. These are your requirements and details:

> Departure date 3 May
> from London, Heathrow to San Francisco, California
> arriving there next day
>
> Mr Terry Porter, Mrs Susanne Porter, Miss Kelly Porter, Master Tim Porter
> 85 Tuddenham Road
> Woodbridge IP32 4TK
> home phone 013943 87943   office phone 01473 290711
>
> 10 nights accommodation at Golden Gate Palace Hotel, San Francisco
> Two double rooms, one with balcony, one with harbour view

21   Here are half of the answers to the airport codes quiz. Your partner has the rest of the answers. Which of the answers did you get right? Which couldn't you guess?

AMS = Amsterdam
BKK = Bangkok
CAI = Cairo
FCO = Rome (Leonardo da
           Vinci/Fiumicino)
GIG = Rio de Janeiro
IST = Istanbul

KUL   = Kuala Lumpur
LHR *or* LGW   = London (Heathrow, Gatwick,
   or STN *or* LCY   Stansted *or* City)
MIA   = Miami
ORD   = Chicago (O'Hare)
SEL   = Seoul
TXL *or* SXF   = Berlin (Tegel or Schönefeld)

> *Ah, ORD is Chicago — I thought so.*
> *I didn't realise that GIG was Rio de Janeiro.*

22   This role play is in four parts so that you both get two turns at filling in the room chart.

1   You are the RESERVATIONS MANAGER at the Royal Hotel. Answer the phone and take the booking. Fill in the room chart on page 56.

2   Your name is ANNIE ANDERSON. Call the Royal Hotel. You want to reserve a room for your sister and yourself from May 6 to May 8 (two nights). You don't want to pay more than $100 for bed and breakfast. (Your home phone number is 01981 83 21 23.)

3   You are the RESERVATIONS MANAGER. Take the booking and fill in the room chart.

4   Your name is DAWN DAVIDSON. Call the hotel to reserve a room for two people from May 2 to May 8. (Your office phone number is 0181 821 4832.)

23 This role play is in two parts so that you both get a turn at answering enquiries. You'll need to spell some of the difficult names aloud to your partner and say the numbers slowly and clearly.

1 You are an INFORMATION OFFICER. Refer to this information to answer your client's questions.

LODGE CONTACT DETAILS
South Island

Motueka River Lodge, PO Box 238, Motueka, New Zealand.
   Tel 64-3-526 8668, fax 64-3-526 8669.

Ilmara Lodge, Dog Point Road, RD 2, Blenheim, Marlborough, New Zealand.
   Tel 64-3-572 8276, fax 64-3-572 9191.

Moonlight Lodge, PO Box 12, Murchison, New Zealand.
   Tel 64-3-523 9323, fax 64-3-523 9515.

Sherwood Lodge, Sherwood Road, RD, Waiau, North Canterbury, New Zealand.
   Tel 64-3-315 6078, fax 64-3-315 6424.

Braemar Lodge, PO Box 89, Hanmer Springs, North Canterbury, New Zealand.
   Tel 64-3-315 7049, fax 64-3-315 7104.

Grasmere Lodge, Private Bag 55009, Christchurch, New Zealand.
   Tel 64-3-318 8407, fax 64-3-318 8263.

Lake Brunner Lodge, Mitchells, RD 1, Kumara 7871, Westland, New Zealand.
   Tel/fax 64-3-738 0163.

Remarkables Lodge, PO Box 144, Wakatipu 9195, Queenstown, New Zealand.
   Tel/fax 64-3-442 2720.

Stewart Island Lodge, PO Box 5, Halfmoon Bay, Stewart Island, New Zealand.
   Tel/fax 64-3-219 1085.

2 Change roles. Now you are a TOURIST. Call the New Zealand Lodge Association and find out the phone numbers for these places:

Okiato Lodge in Russell	....
Kingfish Lodge in Northland	....
Brooklands Country Estate in Waikato	....
Inverness Estate in Papakura	....

and the full addresses for these places:

Muriaroha Lodge	....
Mangapapa Lodge in Hawke's Bay	....
Huka Lodge in Taupo	....
Moose Lodge in Lake Rotoiti	....

24 This role play is in four parts so that you both get two turns at noting down messages.

1 You are a RECEPTIONIST. Take down the message you're given on one of the message pads on page 35. Check that you have noted down all the information correctly.

2 Now you are the CALLER. Leave this message for Julie Stubbs who is a guest at the Bay View Hotel:

> Your name is **Chris Tennant**. Your phone number is **0171 345 9387**. Could Ms Stubbs get in touch with you as soon as possible, please? You'll be at this number till **6pm** and after that she can reach you on your mobile (cellphone): the number is **08978 2847892**.

3 You are the RECEPTIONIST. Take down the message you're given on the other message pad on page 35 Check that you have noted down all the information correctly.

4 Now you are the CALLER again. Leave this message for Tony Priestley, who is a guest at the Bay View Hotel:

> Your name is **Terry Patterson**. Your phone number is **01203 239765**. Mr Priestley's flight has been changed tomorrow: the flight number is still **IC 104**, but it's been retimed to take off at **07.00** instead of 09.00. This means he should check in at **06.00** at the latest. The airline's local number (Icarus Airways) is **2 983 2849**, if he needs to contact them.

25 This role play is in two parts so that you both get a turn at being the waiter/waitress.

1 You are a WAITER/WAITRESS. Add up the bill in the presence of the guest, checking each item as you go through the order. (Make at least one deliberate mistake!)

> So that's two melons — that's three pounds. And two Waldorf salads — that's another nine pounds. Then you had two grilled trout — that's ...

Table 13			Total
2	Melon	@ £1·50	
2	Waldorf salad	@ £4·50	
2	Grilled trout	@ £9·50	
2	Veal schnitzel	@ £11·00	
4	Ice cream	@ £2·40	
1	carafe of white wine	@ £7·50	
2	bottles of beer	@ £1·50	
4	cover charge	@ £2·00	
	+ service 10%		
		Total =	

2 You are the GUEST. You've finished your coffee. Ask the waiter/waitress to bring you your bill. Listen carefully and make sure he or she gets everything right — especially the arithmetic.

26 This role play is in four parts. In the first two parts you are a guest staying at the Hotel Miramar.

1 You are a GUEST at the Hotel Miramar. Ask one of the receptionists to help you with these questions. Here are the things you want to do . . .

find out if you can get to Granada by train. Can you book a room in a good hotel there?

find out how to get to the airport for your flight to Rio Verde.

find out where and when breakfast is served.

2 Now ask a *different* receptionist to help you with these questions. You want to . . .

change your room to one with a better view.

find out how long it takes to get to the international airport.

find out what time you have to check out.

reserve a room for your next visit in a month's time.

3 & 4 Now you are a RECEPTIONIST on duty at the reception desk at the Hotel Miramar. Answer your guest's queries.

•HOTEL•
MIRAMAR INFORMATION

Rooms with a sea view are $95, rooms overlooking the garden are $85. You have only one $95 room available now, but several for next month.

Dinner is served in the Gaucho Grill, Atlantic Restaurant (8–11.30pm) or Roof Top Room on the 20th floor (10pm–3am). Roof Top Room has a cabaret and dancing.

The **swimming pool** (open from 6am to 7pm) is on the roof. Towels available from the attendant (always on duty — press the bell to call him).

Checking out time is 11am. Luggage can be stored for guests who have checked out.

International flights depart from Simón Bolívar Airport (25km from here). Allow 1 hour by taxi + 1 hour to check in.

Domestic flights depart from National Airport (5 km from here) to other cities:

Mendoza: 8.30 14.30

Granada: 10.30 17.30

Rio Verde: 12.00 18.15

Allow 30 minutes by taxi + 45 minutes to check in.

Taxis are normally always available outside the hotel. They cannot be booked in advance.

Today's **exchange rate** is $1 = 1595 pesos.

---

27 Take it in turns to play the roles of guest and member of staff. Keep changing roles. First, you are a guest.

GUEST Explain each of these problems to the member of staff and ask for his or her help.

1 The people in the next room are having a very loud argument and I can't sleep.
2 I'm trying to phone home but I can't get an outside line.
3 I left my briefcase on the balcony and all my documents got wet in the rain.
4 I've just spilt coffee all over my suit. I have an interview this morning.

MEMBER OF STAFF Ask the guest if you can help.

> *I've got a problem . . .*
> *I wonder of you could help me?*

28

This role play is in two parts so that you both get a turn at being the rental clerk.

1 You are a CAR RENTAL CLERK. Refer to this information and fill out the form below for the client.

Cars available today: Group A ($100 per week) Ford Fiesta; Group B (no cars available);
Group C ($145 per week) Ford Escort.
Prices include unlimited mileage.
Full insurance: $12 per day
Return to another location: $20 surcharge

Name . . . .
       title   *first name*   *family name*
Car required: Group . . . . Make . . . .
Full insurance required?   Yes ☐   No ☐
Unlimited mileage?   Yes ☐   No ☐
From . . . .
       time   *day*   *month*   *year*
To . . . .
       time   *day*   *month*   *year*
Pick-up location . . . .
Return location . . . .

2 You are the CLIENT. You want to rent a Group A car at this location. You want to have the car tomorrow at 9am and you'll return it to the airport at the same time one week from then. Find out how much this will cost with unlimited mileage and full insurance.
Begin by saying: *Hello. I'd like to rent a car, please.*

29

This role play is in two parts so that you both get a turn at playing each role.

1 You are a GUEST. Ask the receptionist these questions:

Is there somewhere I can go to hear jazz? Or classical music?
Is there an open-air swimming pool near here?
I need some walking boots. Where can I buy some?
I've got a free afternoon today. What should I do?
I can't decide whether to go to the opera or to the cinema this evening. What do you recommend?

2 You are the RECEPTIONIST. The guest will ask you for some advice.

30

This role play is in two parts so that you both get a turn at being the receptionist. Today is Sunday, May 1st.

1 You are MR or MRS BROWN and you're checking in at the Royal Hotel. You phoned to reserve a room from May 2nd. You have arrived a day early — is there a room for you?

2 You are the RECEPTIONIST at the Royal Hotel. Welcome the guest and go through the check-in procedure. Consult the room chart on page 56.

31

This role play is in two parts so that you both get a turn at playing each role.

1 You are a RECEPTIONIST at the Royal Hotel. Explain to the guest how to get to the places marked on this map of the north of the city.

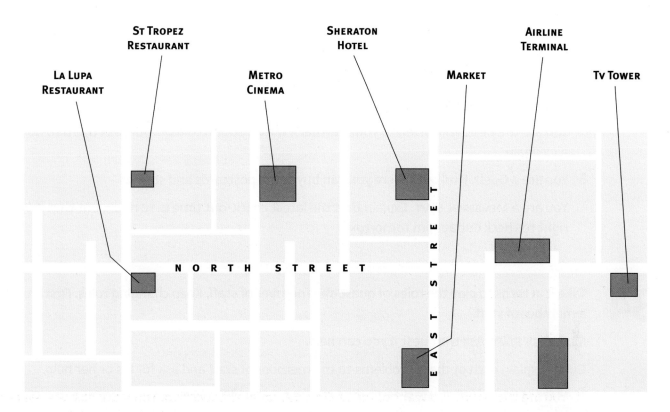

2 You are a GUEST at the Royal Hotel. Ask the receptionist where four of these places are and mark them on the map on page 86.

the Plaza cinema	the castle	the Sears department store
the Hilton Hotel	the Opera House	the Green Parrot restaurant

32

This role play is in two parts so that you both get a turn at being the cashier.

1 You are a CLIENT. Imagine that you don't trust the cashier's arithmetic. Write down the prices the cashier tells you — and make sure he or she gets the final total right.

2 You are the CASHIER. Explain to the client how much he or she has to pay.

Two nights accommodation @ $55 per night	=	
Three lunches @ $19 each	=	
Four dinners @ $29 each	=	
Five bottles of house red @ $11.95 each	=	
Six bottles of mineral water @ $3.50 each	=	
TOTAL	=	

33 In these six short role plays you'll be playing the role of guest or member of staff — or observer. The observer listens to the role play and then gives the others feedback on how polite and friendly they sounded.

1. You are the OBSERVER. Listen to your partners. Tell them how polite, helpful and friendly they sound. If they sound cold or rude, ask them to do the role play again.

2. You are a GUEST. Find out the best way to get from here to the city centre.

3. You are a MEMBER OF STAFF. Explain that the dialling code for the UK is 0044. To get an outside line from your room you need to dial 0 first and wait for the dialling tone.

4. You are the OBSERVER. Listen to your partners. If they sound cold or rude, ask them to do the role play again.

5. You are a GUEST. Find out where you can buy some postcards and stamps.

6. You are a MEMBER OF STAFF. Explain that the latest check-out time is 12 noon, but that it will be all right to check out at 4pm tomorrow.

34 Take it in turns to play the roles of guest and member of staff. Keep changing roles. First, you are a member of staff.

MEMBER OF STAFF Ask the guest if you can help.

GUEST Explain each of these problems to the member of staff and ask for his or her help.

1. *All the lights in my room have suddenly gone out. I've got some important work to finish.*
2. *My empty suitcase has been stolen from my room.*
3. *I want to go for a swim but the pool's closed.*
4. *I've missed my flight because I overslept.*

> *I have a problem . . .*
> *I wonder if you could help me?*

35 Take it in turns to play the roles of guest and member of staff. Keep changing roles. First, you are a member of staff.

GUEST Make each of these complaints to the member of staff.

1. *The piped music in the restaurant is driving me mad.*
2. *The air-conditioning in my room isn't working.*
3. *My soup is cold.*
4. *I booked a room with a view but this one overlooks the car park.*
5. *The brochure says you have a 'large swimming pool', but it's very small.*
6. *I told you yesterday that my TV doesn't work, but no one has come to fix it.*

MEMBER OF STAFF Deal with the complaints politely and apologetically.

36

Here is some extra information about the three places described on page 65.

Club St. Lucia

Club St. Lucia By Splash is a lively, fun hotel with excellent family facilities and unbeatable prices, making this superior medium class hotel a popular choice with Kuoni clients last year. The adults only village makes this a great choice for wedding couples and honeymooners too!

Minimum stay: 7 nights, Dec 22–Jan 03.

Anse Chastanet

This is a truly unique superior first class hideaway resort in one of the most romantic settings we know, with breathtaking scenery. Ideal for honeymooners, escapists, nature lovers and scuba divers, for those seeking a tranquil hideaway or those seeking an active outdoor holiday.

Meal supplements per night: HB Apr 06–Dec 21 £30, FB Jan 01–Apr 05 £16, Apr 06–Dec 21 £46, Dec 22–Dec 31 £17, ALL Jan 01–Apr 05 £32, Apr 06–Dec 21 £62, Dec 22–Dec 31 £34.

East Winds Inn

Guests may find the approach road somewhat bumpy but East Winds is private and enchanting – this relaxed, intimate first class hotel is expertly and personally managed and the perfect tropical escape.

No children under 12 allowed Feb 01–Mar 06.

Prices

7 nights all-inclusive 16 Jul–27 Aug, per person (based on on two sharing)

East Winds Inn		extra night	single supplement per night
SUP	£1633	£120	£75
DLX	£1766	£139	£75
OV	£1766	£139	£75
Anse Chastanet		extra night	single supplement per night
SUP	£1399	£90	£59
BCH	£1553	£112	£73
DLX	£1658	£127	£59
Club St. Lucia		extra night	single supplement per night
STD	£1262	£67	£67
SAV	£1283	£70	£70
ROM	£1283	£70	£70
FMS	£1332	£77	£77
DOV	£1444	£93	£93

Flights

BWIA Airbus 340

Ex Heathrow
TUE/SUN daylight flight

Ex St Lucia
TUE/SUN overnight flight

37

These are model notes for the two telephone messages on pages 34 and 35.

~ PHOENIX HOTEL ~

DATE AND TIME [today's date & time now]

MESSAGE FOR Reservations

FROM KATHERINE WOODFORD TEL. NO. 893 89 82 40

FAX. NO. 893 34 56 25

Ms Woodford wants 2 double rooms + shower + balconies for Feb 14th for 2 nights

Please confirm by fax, or phone before 9pm

[your name]

Newtown-on-sea
INFORMATION BUREAU

Date and time [today's date & time now]

Message for Reception

From TIM HUGHES

Tel. No. ?

Mr Hughes has room booked for 12 Feb.

Arriving very late. Please hold the room –

Visa no. 7777 1902 2867 3456 exp 12/02

Also please send brochure to:

SONIA BLAKE 1232 Forest Drive, Fargo

ND 58105

[your name]

38 Read this letter and the reply below. Highlight the useful phrases in the reply which you can use in your own letter of apology.

91 Richmond Avenue
Bournemouth BH3 4TH

Utopia Holidays
Utopia House
Airways Drive
Horsham RH4 9LK

21 October [year]

Dear Sirs,

We have recently returned from a weekend break in New York with Utopia Holidays. Our enjoyment was seriously spoiled by the low quality of the Rotterdam Hotel and its facilities.

Our room was clean and newly decorated, but it was very cold and there were repeated problems with the hot water, so that we were unable to have a warm shower on several occasions. When we complained at the front desk about this we were told that the boiler was out of order and "being fixed". We were offered extra blankets to keep us warm in bed. The television in our room was very old and only showed four channels.

Although the hotel is in a fine central position, it is very run down and once you have left the lobby to make your way upstairs, the corridors are dirty and dark.

We urge you not to use the Rotterdam Hotel again.

Yours faithfully,

Hannah Rosser

Mrs H. Rosser

Utopia Holidays

UTOPIA HOUSE ✦ AIRWAYS DRIVE ✦ HORSHAM RH4 9LK

Mrs Hannah Rosser
91 Richmond Avenue
Bournemouth BH3 4TH

14 November [year]

Dear Mrs Rosser

Many thanks for your letter dated 21st October.

It is our wish, of course, that all our clients thoroughly enjoy their holidays and that all aspects are entirely to their satisfaction. I was very sorry to hear of your dissatisfaction with certain aspects of your recent holiday.

It is sometimes difficult for us to keep completely up to date with all the hotels featured in our brochures, and so we rely primarily on the hotel to advise us of any changes or reductions in facilities. We also strongly welcome feedback from our clients to keep us accurately informed. Your comments have been noted with extreme concern and are now being taken up with Management at the property. I cannot apologise enough for the disappointment that you experienced.

In view of the problems you incurred on this occasion, I would like to offer you compensation of £50.00 per person. Our cheque for the sum of £100.00 is enclosed in full and final settlement. I hope you will accept this with my sincere apologies.

Despite your recent experience, I hope that you will allow us to assist with your travel arrangements again as we would welcome the chance to restore your faith in our services and I am certain you would not be disappointed.

As a gesture of goodwill and a token of our apologies on this occasion, I have enclosed a 10% discount voucher which can be used against your next Utopia Holiday. Should you wish to take advantage of this offer, please contact me directly and I will personally deal with your travel arrangements.

Thank you for taking the time to write to us. I hope that despite some dissatisfaction you enjoyed your Utopia Holiday and that we will have the pleasure of welcoming you back again soon.

Yours sincerely
UTOPIA HOLIDAYS LIMITED

Anna Brown

Anna Brown
Customer Services Manager